Many times when you read a book that has a great effect on you, you don't know the author. In this case I do. I have also watched the manifestation of truth that Watch of the Lord so beautifully delivers. It is the heart of God. I believe that every family, church and nation should read this book. We as a people need to be constant watchmen, looking into the distance, observing, awaiting, always aware of how God works importantly in our lives. This book gives direction, focus and inspiration as to how to see God's power and glory.

—AL KASHA
TWO-TIME ACADEMY AWARD-WINNING
SONGWRITER AND PRODUCER

Mahesh Chavda has for many years been a man of deep prayer and fasting and has personally experienced the breakthrough in God that follows. His book will inspire you to pursue the benefits of corporate prayer, as in the Watch of the Lord, as well as a personal prayer life hidden in God. I highly recommend this book.

—JOHN ARNOTT, SENIOR PASTOR
TORONTO AIRPORT CHRISTIAN FELLOWSHIP

Mahesh and Bonnie Chavda not only present a compelling reason for the Watch of the Lord, but they live it. It is part of their DNA.

—CHÉ AHN, SENIOR PASTOR
HARVEST ROCK CHURCH
PASADENA, CALIFORNIA

The Holy Spirit is awakening those who are part of the slumbering bride of Christ to come and take their places as watchmen on the walls in this hour. Few today have the knowledge, experience and impartation that Mahesh and Bonnie Chavda have in this arena. This book is more than a technical exposé on biblical principles. Watch of the Lord contains a highly contagious virus of the Holy Spirit that will ruin you from living a mediocre Christian life. Read this book and you will be hooked into God's purposes as an End-Time watchman in His army.

—JIM GOLL
MINISTRY TO THE NATIONS
AUTHOR OF THE LOST ART OF INTERCESSION
AND KNEELING ON THE PROMISES

Intimacy with God, the presence of the Lord and a passion for Jesus are buzz phrases in Christianity today. But to Mahesh and Bonnie Chavda, they are reality. Watch of the Lord *has made these phrases a reality to me and the church I pastor. If your heart burns for this to be real for you, this is a must-read book!*

—Tim Burgan
Producer, Cornerstone Television, Pittsburgh, PA
Senior Producer, *His Place* and *Getting Together*
Pastor, Indian Lake Christian Center

The Watch of the Lord was birthed by the Spirit of God in the hearts of pastors Mahesh and Bonnie Chavda several years ago. Now, many churches all over the world are keeping the Watch of the Lord with all-night praise, worship, prayer and intercession. As we present our bodies as a living sacrifice in prayer, obedience and holiness to God, our prayers will release angels to go where we cannot go.

I have had the privilege of attending several prayer watches in Charlotte. The first time I walked into the church building to be a part of the watch, the overwhelming presence of the Lord and the spirit of intercession were very evident. I was also blessed to be one of the many watchmen from around the world who passed the night in prayer at the Wailing Wall with the Chavdas in Jerusalem. The impartation and enrichment I have received in my own life and walk with the Lord through these corporate prayer watches have helped to take me deeper and higher in my own personal prayer time.

—Suzanne Hinn, Intercessor
World Outreach Church
Orlando, FL

Mahesh and Bonnie Chavda stepped into the timing of the Lord and began to organize prayer watches across America and in other nations. They are both people of the spirit of Issachar, knowing the timings and seasons of the Lord. As you read their book, you will not only feel the Holy Spirit's urgency of the hour, but also know how to respond. They are experienced people you can trust.

—Ruth Ward Heflin
Director, Calvary Pentecostal Tabernacle
Ashland, VA

Watch
of the *Lord*®

MAHESH AND BONNIE CHAVDA

WATCH OF THE LORD by Mahesh and Bonnie Chavda
Published by Creation House
A part of Strang Communications Company
600 Rinehart Road
Lake Mary, FL 32746
www.creationhouse.com

Unless otherwise noted, all Scripture quotations are from the New King James
Version of the Bible. Copyright © 1979, 1980, 1982 by
Thomas Nelson, Inc., publishers. Used by permission.

Scripture quotations marked KJV are from the King James Version of the Bible.

Scripture quotations marked NIV are from the Holy Bible, New International
Version. Copyright © 1973, 1978, 1984, International Bible Society.
Used by permission.

Scripture quotations marked NAS are from the New American Standard Bible.
Copyright © 1960, 1962, 1963, 1968, 1971, 1972, 1973, 1975, 1977
by the Lockman Foundation. Used by permission.

Scripture quotations marked AMP are from the Amplified Bible. Old Testament
copyright © 1965, 1987 by the Zondervan Corporation. The Amplified New
Testament copyright © 1954, 1958, 1987 by the Lockman Foundation.
Used by permission.

Scripture quotations marked NCV are from The Holy Bible, New Century Version.
Copyright © 1987, 1988, 1991 by Word Publishing, Dallas, TX 75039.
Used by permission.

Scripture quotations marked NLT are from the Holy Bible, New Living
Translation, copyright © 1996. Used by permission of Tyndale House
Publishers, Inc., Wheaton, IL 60189. All rights reserved.

Library of Congress Cataloging-in-Publication Data
Chavda, Mahesh, 1946–
    Watch of the Lord / by Mahesh and Bonnie Chavda.
        p. cm.
    ISBN 0-88419-562-7
    1. Prayer—Christianity. 2. Second Advent. I. Chavda, Bonnie. II. Title.
BV227.C48 1999
269—dc21   99-32779
                                                                    CIP

0 1 2 3 4 5 6 BBG 9 8 7 6 5 4 3
Printed in the United States of America

We lovingly dedicate this book to the Supreme Commander of the watch, the Lord Jesus Christ; to our four children: Ben, Anna, Serah and Aaron, who have shared in our adventures of faith; and to all the watchmen at our base in Charlotte who have faithfully kept the Watch of the Lord.

Acknowledgments

Thanks go to our faithful staff:
Steve Martin, Karen Johnston, Marian Duffee,
Leslie Adams and Lorraine Runyans.
May the Lord reward you for your
dedication and faithful service.

Contents

Foreword

§

I T IS MY privilege to commend this book to you, for it will open dimensions of prayer that will challenge, encourage and thrill you.

Mahesh Chavda has been in the ministry for more than twenty-five years. I have known Mahesh and his gifted wife, Bonnie, personally for fifteen years. They are dear friends and anointed servants of God who personify their message. I jokingly refer to Mahesh as a "workhorse" in the Charismatic movement as opposed to a "show horse." His servant spirit is an example to us all. Mahesh and Bonnie exemplify hard work, and they have persevered in prayer for many years. They have been a source of encouragment to me, to our church and to thousands of others who have begun to watch and pray because of their example and teaching.

In this book they not only share their adventures in the exciting realm of watching and praying, but they have distilled all the wisdom they have gleaned from helping to birth and lead the Watch of the Lord over the last several years. More than five hundred churches and prayer groups are linked to their prayer network; more are being added weekly. Hundreds of thousands of hours of intercession are going up monthly as a result of this extraordinary prayer movement.

This book is timely and strategic. I have been richly blessed by their other books, but this book may be their greatest contribution to the body of Christ. Their revelation from the Book of Ruth of the church's bridal relationship with Christ, encouraging intimacy with the Lord as our Boaz through the watch, deeply touched my heart.

You will not only be challenged as I was, but you will receive many practical steps to do the Watch of the Lord yourself. Because Mahesh and Bonnie Chavda have experienced this and led thousands in watching, there is a living impartation through this book.

We are on the threshold of a new millennium. The Chavdas are postured as few others to make a prophetic trumpet blast, calling the millennial church across the globe to obey the Lord's call to "watch and pray."

—MIKE BICKLE, FOUNDER
FRIENDS OF THE BRIDEGROOM MINISTRIES

PART I

§

*The glory of this latter house shall be greater than of the former, saith the L*ORD *of hosts: and in this place will I give peace, saith the L*ORD *of hosts.*

—HAGGAI 2:9, KJV

1

The Birth of the Watch

§

THE PIERCING BLAST of a shofar tears through the atmosphere, and adults, teenagers and children shout their praises toward heaven as if asking God to send His glory down. It's ten o'clock on Friday evening in Charlotte, North Carolina, and the Watch of the Lord has begun.

About one hundred fifty people have gathered at All Nations Church, the church we started in Charlotte in 1994. Each Friday night "watchmen" from Charlotte and the surrounding area—from near and far, actually—join us as we stay awake all night, praying and waiting upon the Lord. We always begin with the blast of the shofar (ram's horn), followed by energetic praise and worship. Yet, while we begin each watch the same way, no two watches are ever the same.

The matchless creativity of God is ever present. Though some aspects of the watch are fixed—the praise, the intimacy with Jesus, the global prayer concerns—the current of the Spirit inevitably engulfs us, taking us on a special journey in His wonderful river, moving from glory to glory.

Since 1995 we have been spending Friday nights like this—on dates with Jesus. They get better and better. But let me tell you how it all started.

TAKE BACK THE LAND

IN MARCH 1986 I was at the House of Representatives in Washington, D.C., leading a national prayer seminar with Intercessors for America. I was in the middle of a forty-day fast at that time, and the Lord visited me nightly during my stay in Washington.

One night, the Lord took me in the spirit above the earth. My spirit was as high as a satellite; from that vantage point, I saw the nations. Fires were exploding across different parts of the world, and I knew these were the fires of revival. I saw that Great Britain and Germany were destined to experience revival and to help in the evangelism and shepherding of the nations. These Holy Spirit fires of revival were also bursting forth in different locations in the United States; from there they spread across the nation.

Some of the major fires I saw falling in the United States were in the inner cities, in integrated groups of African Americans, Hispanics and other cultures and peoples meeting together. That seemed to be a pleasing mixture to the heart of God, like the blending of cultures and denominations that occurred in the Azusa Street revival at the beginning of the century. After all, He is the Lord of all nations and all peoples. The Lord gave me the words *humble, holy* and *hungry* to describe the people who would be the first recipients of His visitation.

My heart has always been toward the poor and broken of the Third World. I have focused much of my attention, time and resources there. I have conducted many evangelistic meetings in Africa and Asia, laid my hands on thousands and seen many miracles. Yet, as one of America's adopted sons, I feel a great debt of gratitude to this nation and have for years yearned to see a visitation of God in this country. That day in my hotel room the Lord revealed to me a key to His glory coming to America.

> "I have called you to be a missionary to America," He said. "I have made fasting and prayer a living truth in your life. Now go through this nation to impart this gift and train the thousands I will show you. Satan wants to destroy America from the inside out and has built many evil strongholds over it. Yet it is My will that from America a mighty thrust of the gospel goes forth to all nations. When this happens, Satan's time will be up. He wants to delay the end as long as possible, so he plans to weaken and destroy this nation.
>
> "The work of believers who are willing to pay the price of prayer and fasting will hold back Satan's hordes and foil his strategies. America will remain strong through united fasting and prayer—the only sure means of driving out evil spirits."

Suddenly I could see it clearly: The key to victory over the evil strongholds of secular humanism, racism, abortion, drugs, divorce, pornography, child abuse and violence was to wield the spiritual weapons of intercession and fasting until the strongholds fell and revival came to America. Also, I realized that God had commissioned me to recruit others for the fight.

As in an Olympic relay race, the baton was being passed to America to fulfill her destiny in the last days—to bring the light of the Lord, the gospel, to the nations.

CONFIRMATION BY GOD

WHAT I DID not realize was that as God was speaking to me in Washington, simultaneously He was speaking to my wife, Bonnie, at our home in Fort Lauderdale, Florida. At that time we had four small children. Bonnie awoke one night to find the lights on in the house. Knowing that she had turned them all out when she went to bed, she assumed one of the children was up, so she arose to investigate.

Coming into the living room, she found that the light was not coming from any electric lamp, but from a thick sense of the living presence of God, as though He had stopped by our home to visit at that hour and was waiting to be greeted and welcomed.

As Bonnie knelt on the carpet before His presence, God spoke to her about revival in America. Over the next few nights, instead of sleeping, Bonnie kept the Watch of the Lord, just sitting awake in His presence, being washed and renewed by Him as she worshiped. The Lord gave her visions as well as some specific instructions. He told Bonnie all about the latter rain that was coming—just as prophesied in the Book of Joel—and how prayer would help prepare the way for this new wave of revival that was coming to America.

For a long time Bonnie and I had been crying out to God for the day when He would come to His people and reside with them! Even when I was a pastor in Levelland, Texas, in 1974, around the time Bonnie and I were married, we would watch and pray once a month with others from the church and neighboring areas. We see now that even then we were hungry for global revival. And now the Lord was confirming His plans to Bonnie and me separately, giving us a strategy to welcome His presence.

A POWERFUL VISITATION

WHEN I ARRIVED home from Washington, Bonnie and I compared notes. We discovered that we had been given the same message from God regarding our church: God wanted us to come before Him in fasting and prayer. Bonnie had the word that we should begin a twenty-day fast. I felt that we were to meet for prayer daily from 5 A.M. to 7 A.M. during that time.

At the time Bonnie and I were associate pastors with Dr. Derek Prince at our church in Fort Lauderdale. We presented this message to the church board, who agreed that it was a word from God. The people willingly and readily responded to the message as well, and many fasted—some for the whole twenty-one days and others for a portion of it. During the entire twenty-one-day period, believers

4

were ministering to God in an unbroken chain of twenty-four-hour fasting, prayer, praise and worship.

As we met together, we saw signs and wonders, repentance, salvation, deliverance, revelation and divine visitation for everyone from ages five to eighty-five. Together, we experienced an unusual, corporate, supernatural presence of God that was unsurpassed. Dr. Derek Prince recalls that whole time as being the greatest manifestation of God's presence he had yet experienced in his then forty-plus years of ministry.

During those early morning watches, God revealed Himself at times in corporate open visions the likes of which I've never experienced before or since. One day several people saw a cross in the middle of the sanctuary, with the blood and the redemptive power flowing out of it. The literal presence of God hovered over us in those meetings. Bonnie and I wept as we felt awe and fear in such breathtaking holiness and glory. And we were not alone.

Some of the people in our church, even those who were thought to be models of integrity, had been keeping a form of religion, but their inward fire had gone out. They were in a wilderness, having been taken over by other loves, from television to alcoholism to pornography. The cloud of the Lord's presence brought those things to the surface in people's lives. Suddenly, people were getting a living drink of God's presence. Those other waters were muddy waters of which they no longer wanted to partake. No one was even preaching repentance, yet this revelation was coming in waves in every meeting! More and more people were coming, falling on their faces and weeping before the Lord.

During this powerful visitation, the Lord spoke many things to us regarding what is yet to come within the body of Christ. He said the Charismatic movement was in danger of developing its own rigid traditions and the same deadness that had permeated prior movements. "My presence will lift, and you won't even realize it if you do not learn how to recognize, value and steward the cloud of My presence when I come into your midst," the Lord warned.

This visitation was what we had been seeking. It was glorious to be in the literal presence of God, being washed and refreshed. But after a couple of months, some people became uneasy with the continual repentance; they were disturbed that people were so openly distraught about their sins. They wanted to move on from repentance to celebration. We have since learned that when people react to what the Lord is doing instead of participating in it, the Lord can feel uninvited and will leave.

Looking back, we can see that the Lord wasn't finished yet with our repentance. We believe that God wanted us to move from personal repentance to repenting for our families, our cities and our nations. Daniel fasted, prayed and humbled himself before God on behalf of his people, saying, "We have sinned and committed iniquity" (Dan. 9:5). We also are called to repent on behalf of others.

In trying to celebrate before we finished with what God was doing, we left God behind, and His presence and anointing slowly faded. After a time, the congregation returned to business as usual.

SORROW IN OUR HEARTS

THIS UNIQUE VISITATION waned, leaving us hungry and thirsty for more of the same heavenly outpouring of God's Spirit. Those who had been touched by God as the heavens opened were forever impacted—how we missed Him!

The Bible says that the latter house will be greater than the former house (Hag. 2:9). Great signs, wonders and miracles were experienced in a large degree in the former house—in biblical times. Why are there not many miracles performed today? One reason is that the church has lost her faith in the miraculous; for centuries many seminaries have taught that the gift of miracles passed away with the deaths of the original twelve apostles. So if it is true that the glory of the latter house—the church of today—is to be greater than that of the former house, the Lord must teach us first about His glory and how to receive and sustain it.

Once you taste the glory of God, you will want more. Once the glory is manifest in your presence, you will want to know how to steward it properly so that it resides and does not depart. Bonnie and I carried sorrow in our hearts; God's manifest glory had lifted. We felt as though this living "baby" of His presence had died prematurely. However difficult, we prepared to receive and welcome Him when He came again.

A HEART OF EXPECTATION

WE WENT ON with our ministry work in the Third World, praying and fasting as usual, maintaining a heart of expectation, never giving up. We continued to expect and to prepare for His presence because we knew then, as we do now, that He is a wonderful God who loves us. His heart is always one of loving us and wanting the best for us.

Many people have an image of God that makes them tense, such as the tension you may experience when you know you are about to feel pain. The religious way of looking at God is as a hard, angry taskmaster who wants to beat up on us more than He wants to bless us. This concept will tighten you up. Not only is it inaccurate, but it also leaves you with a closed heart instead of an expectant heart.

Those of us who have been in the religious system for the last ten years or more have been conditioned to expect God to come with judgment and anger. That's one of the reasons the recent renewal wasn't recognized immediately as being from God—it didn't fit in with what our religious traditions had taught us about what to expect when the Lord visited next. Many of us had an image in our minds of what the answer to our prayers for revival would look like. For most of us, this spiritual renewal was not it!

But it was the beginning of God's answer. How like the Lord to send goodness and mercy instead of first raining down fire and judgment! God showed up His way, and whole nations are being impacted. But just as the Pharisees didn't recognize Jesus coming as a servant instead of a king, some of us still miss moves of God because they don't fit into our limited expectation.

The Lord wants to love His bride, to woo His bride. When you are wooing, you don't beat up your bride. The heavenly Father is not abusive with His children. He is good and is a *rewarder* of those who diligently seek Him (Heb. 11:6). His goodness is beyond any human description. To cultivate expectation, you need a heart full of love and adoration toward the Lord, and that comes by knowing how much He loves and adores you.

"OCCUPY TILL I COME"

SO WE CONTINUED to pray and fast. We have learned that fasting, even if it's one day a week or one day a month, helps prepare our hearts for Him. Everything we had—all our treasures—were invested in the kingdom. We went to many countries on several continents and preached the gospel, witnessing signs and wonders, miracles and salvations. We were completely immersed in aggressively preaching the gospel to the poor, with signs following. All of our resources, our desires, our dreams and our goals were being invested consistently in advancing His kingdom.

Perhaps you are not in full-time ministry. It makes no difference at all in your devotion to Christ. You can focus your prayers and resources toward getting the gospel out. Do things of practical service, whether in the church body or in helping others go to the nations. There's no reason for anybody in America to say, "I can't help." If you can't go, you can help someone else to go.

Jesus said, "Occupy till I come" (Luke 19:13, KJV). In short, that's what we did.

Over time, the Lord added to us people who had the same vision we did. Some who could not go to the mission field as Bonnie and I could helped by taking care of our children, praying or aiding us in other ways. This made it practical for us to go and preach the gospel. Those precious people were just as much a part of going as we were. They had their jobs here in America, but their hearts were in missions.

Over the years I saw how wonderfully God blessed them, kept their children from ungodliness and made their children successful because of their giving hearts. The glory touched their children, too, with blessings, protection and success.

8

THE LORD VISITS US AGAIN

DURING THAT SEASON of corporate visitation in Fort Lauderdale, the Holy Spirit conceived within us a precious seed—one that would someday be birthed into what is now the Watch of the Lord. In July 1994 we moved our ministry base to Charlotte and established All Nations Church. During the first month there, the Lord came knocking on the doors of our hearts, asking us to come aside and spend some time with Him, to watch and pray. This was totally unexpected, but we cherished and nurtured it. The Bridegroom was calling for our fellowship, and we were thrilled.

Bonnie and I individually, not even necessarily together, answered the Lord's fresh call to come aside and wait on Him—to have a date with Him. We spent time with Him during the day, welcoming Him as we did our daily tasks. If we choose to believe and ask Him to be with us every day, in every moment, He is there. From time to time I like to acknowledge that He is present, that He is welcome. He is definitely the wonderful One who is most welcome in our house, and I want Him to know it. We are always open to hearing from Him, even expecting to hear from Him.

As we spent time with Him during the day, the manifest glory of the cloud of His presence became tangible. Supernatural things were starting to happen in our lives and in our own household.

At that time we had friends coming and going; they were people who had been with us in our work of taking the gospel to the nations. Some of these people came to visit us after we moved. At that time, the Lord Himself, in His glorious manifest presence, began to come into the house—in the living room, in our sun room, in the kitchen—as if He were coming near to observe what He was doing with us.

People would be chatting with us, when suddenly the spirit of prayer and prophecy would come. The presence of God would simply be there, surrounding everyone. We were drawn into God's presence, and His glory began to thicken. Normal fellowship became corporate prayer time with four, six or twelve people around the cloud of His anointed presence in our house. The prophetic gifts would come, and people would receive visions or words of knowledge from the Lord about things happening internationally or in others' lives.

OH, THE GLORY OF HIS PRESENCE!

AFTER THIS HAPPENED to us a few times, we learned to yield to the Holy Spirit and go right into prayer. The weight of His manifest glory was so intense among us at times that it was impossible to stand during some of these times of prayer. We had to kneel or crawl just in order to move around the house!

Bonnie describes His glory, His manifest presence, like this:

> As His presence comes in, it's like being in a place where the dew falls early in the morning or in the evening. The air becomes moist and ionized. It's literally different from noontime air. The same sense of dew falling is what happens in the realm of the spirit when the Lord's presence comes near.
>
> In Job 14 there's a passage about a stump of a tree that's been cut down. "Though its root may grow old in the earth, and its stump may die in the ground, yet at the scent of water it will bud and bring forth branches like a plant" (vv. 8–9). To me, that's what the presence of the Lord does—it revives. When He draws near and starts manifesting Himself, something in the human soul is like that dry root suddenly getting water.
>
> "Deep calls unto deep at the noise of Your waterfalls; all Your waves and billows have gone over me" (Ps. 42:7). The presence of the Person of the Lord is like water to the human soul—deep calling unto deep.
>
> When I become aware of Him, when something quickens in me the reality of His momentary presence, I respond by saying, "Ah! Hello, Lord! You're welcome here! If You're here, I'm stopping everything to spend time with You and see what's on Your mind."
>
> Once I became sensitized to His presence, it became much

easier to recognize. Sometimes I glimpse Him, so to speak, with my spirit, sensing that His dew is suddenly here for me. I have hope; I have peace. I have a sense of the Lord's nearness, that He's engaged in listening to my prayers and concerned about the needs of my heart right then. When He draws near, and I give myself to His presence more and more, it becomes easier and easier to discern.

Day after day, this visitation of the Lord continued. We wanted to pray all the time. It was our number-one priority. Sometimes I left for ministry trips, and I would return home to find bodies on the floor and people laughing—drunk in the Holy Spirit!

As a result of these times of visitation, we decided to set aside at least one day a week for prayer. These "outbreaks" of prayer and prophecy would usually last from two to six hours each. We began to recognize the Lord's presence and to make room for Him.

Then we thought, *If God is coming as He did in 1986 in Fort Lauderdale, why not call His people to His sanctuary?* We mentioned this to a few people who we knew were really hungry and thirsty for more of the Lord. We decided to use our little chapel, originally a garage, and to meet late on Friday night when people were off work and could come.

THE CORPORATE WATCH IS BIRTHED

THOSE WATCHES (FASTING from sleep for spiritual reasons) soon grew to seventy people crammed into that little chapel. The watches were wonderful visitations from the Lord with miracles, healings, prophetic words and songs from heaven. People's lives were refreshed, revitalized, cleansed and focused.

About a year after we started the Friday night watches, the Lord gave Bonnie a vision. Here it is in her own words:

I was sitting in the living room of our house. Suddenly the Lord came as though from behind me and stuck His right arm (the

11

arm of intercession, strength and favor) in front of my face. I was staring at His hand, wrist and forearm as though it were the arm of a man before my eyes. His skin was tanned as one who labored in the sun. Immediately, this let me know He was hard at work in His vineyard—in the soil of the hearts of men and women on the earth.

However, there was a place around His wrist in the distinct shape of a wristwatch, where the skin had not been darkened by the sun. Obviously, He usually wore His watch there and had done so habitually for a long time. But the watch itself was missing.

He said, "My watch is being repaired." His tone was not casual—it was crucial. Most of us are accustomed to managing our affairs efficiently and successfully throughout the day by referring often to our watches. The Lord showed me that it is the same with Him and His affairs on the earth—in individual lives as well as in destinies of nations. All of it takes referring to His timepiece: the work of intercession mixed with the will of God in heaven, then made manifest on the earth.

I understood His words to mean that He had His watch in "for repairs." It had ceased working—God's house of prayer had become a place for all other kinds of business except real communion in the intimate knowledge of Him. The timetable and events of people and nations had been thrown off schedule— out of sync in some way—because of the lack of Holy Ghost-accomplished prayer.

I knew that He was repairing the inner workings of this critical timepiece—the "watch." Some of His plans had completely ground to a halt because of the absence of a remnant of people who were given to vigilant watching in prayer, as Jesus did while He was on earth.

I also understood that in a little while this "watch" timepiece would be repaired, and when it was, He would strap it back on His right hand of favor and blessing, and things would get back on track; things would start ticking everywhere again. He was getting ready to do something in the earth connected with the Watch of the Lord that would make everything in His prophetic purposes begin to operate on schedule.

It was apparent that God has His watchmen—those vigilant in His true purposes in prayer—very involved in the affairs of every age, now specifically in ours. He has things that are waiting and dependent upon our reinhabiting the great work of old—the watch of prayer!

Meanwhile, the watch continued to grow. We were renovating a horse barn on our property to use as a gathering place. When that was completed, we moved the watch there. I use the word *renovate* loosely. We had no air conditioning in the summer; we used large fans and kept the doors open for airflow, so a lot of insects joined in the watch. In the winter, space heaters were all that we had for heat. It was still quite primitive, and it reminded me of the "barn" or stable in which Jesus was born. Now, two thousand years later, the Watch of the Lord was born in a barn.

Two years later, the Friday night watches moved to our church, All Nations Church. Today, these watch services from week to week are a fresh, corporate experience of Jesus as our Bridegroom Lover, with us, the church, as His bride and army.

THE MISSING LINK

EACH FRIDAY NIGHT we pray, fast and worship together. For a little while we forget our individual ministry agendas, our personal visions and our individual priorities. We put our lives down for a few hours, and for that brief period of time we cease to be Mahesh and Bonnie Chavda. The other prayer warriors who have gathered together to pray do likewise. We lay down our own agendas and pick up God's agenda. We lay down our individuality and pick up a corporate identity. For eight hours we become the bride of Christ.

As you'll find out, the watch is not burdensome at all. It is full of joy, triumph and God's glory. It's both an intimate date with Jesus and a powerful strike into the enemy's territory. We believe the Watch of the Lord is the missing link between the spiritual renewal we have been experiencing and the End-Time harvest. Let me say that again. Many people have wondered about the spiritual renewal and where the harvest of souls might be. It is coming. We are commissioned to bring in the harvest with the help of the Watch of the Lord.

EQUIP, PREPARE AND RELEASE

BONNIE AND I are committed to equip, prepare and release End-Time watchmen on the wall of prayer. The battle is great. Sporadic outbursts of prayer will not accomplish God's objectives for America or the world in this hour. We are calling Christians in every city to respond to God's induction call. Our vision is to see a Watch of the Lord established in every town and city around the globe. And for every family, a watchman intercessor.

When God led us into the Watch of the Lord, we felt that during the first year we should not advertise it publicly. We watched and prayed with people close to us, and it spread by word of mouth. We believed that we had to live it first, then we could pass it on. That was in 1995; at this writing, five hundred watches have been established that are linked with us across the United States and in countries around the world, such as Japan, Israel, Kenya, India, Belize, Egypt, Taiwan, Bolivia, Germany, Malaysia, Congo, Bahrain, Belau (formerly known as Palau), Great Britain and many more. We hold several conferences a year, and over and over people are moved by God to start watches when they return home. There are hundreds of other watches that we don't hear from on a regular basis.

Bonnie and I are convinced that the day is coming when we will not only taste the glory, but it will reside with us and not depart. The day is coming when the Lord will permanently manifest His glory among His people.

At no other time in history has it been as vitally important as it is now for the body of Christ to assume its strategic position on the wall of prayer as God's spiritual watchmen. We believe that the necessary ingredient to bring forth God's glory and power is the watch with prayer, according to the pattern outlined for us biblically.

Jesus, the patriarchs, the prophets and the "great crowd of witnesses" who have gone before us kept and valued the watch in their earthly ministries. Let's learn from them now.

§

WATCH, n: the act of keeping awake to guard, protect or attend; (obsolete) the state of being wakeful; . . . a state of alert and continuous attention.

—WEBSTER'S DICTIONARY

2

The Watch in Scripture

THROUGHOUT SCRIPTURE THERE is evidence of God's power being released when people went without sleep (watched) and prayed—both individually and in one accord with others. Yet it is telling that in Webster's dictionary the definition of a watch as "the state of being wakeful" is termed obsolete.[1] Good thing it wasn't obsolete in biblical times because, as we will see, watches yielded much fruit.

WATCHES IN THE OLD TESTAMENT

THE BIBLICAL PATTERN of watching in the Old Testament was often that of mourning and desperation because of events or seasons of desolation and despair. These events, such as captivity, threats from enemies and natural disasters, caused the people to see their desperate need for God and then turn to Him.

According to Strong's concordance, two main Hebrew words are used for *watch* in the Old Testament. One is *mishmereth,* which implies the act of watching or the post itself. It is a duty, a charge, an office, a safeguard. *Mishmereth* is the feminine form of *mishmar,* which means "diligence, guard...watch." Both these words are derived from *shamar,* a primary root word indicating actions, such as to hedge about (as with thorns), to protect, attend, be circumspect, take heed, keep, mark, look narrowly, observe, preserve, save, lay wait for and watch.

The Hebrew word for *watchman* is also revealing. It is *tsaphah,* meaning "to lean forward...to peer into the distance...to observe, await...behold, espy, look up...wait for, [keep the] watch."

Jacob and the angel

Jacob felt trepidation about seeing Esau, his brother whom he had tricked out of his inheritance, so he watched all night.

> Then Jacob was left alone; and a Man [angel] wrestled with him until the breaking of the day....And He said, "Let Me go, for the day breaks."
> But he said, "I will not let You go unless You bless me!"
> So He said to him, "What is your name?"
> He said, "Jacob."
> And He said, "Your name shall no longer be called Jacob, but Israel; for you have struggled with God and with men, and have prevailed."
> —GENESIS 32:24–28

Wrestling with the angel was not the heart of this account. The true conclusion of this watch in Jacob's life was that the Lord changed his name from Jacob, which meant "supplanter" or "deceiver," to Israel, "a prince before God" or "one who has authority before God." Therefore, because Jacob persevered and watched throughout the night and wrestled with the angel, the Lord transformed his identity.

In our watches, we also tell God, "We are not going to let You go.

We are going to lay hold of Your garments, Lord. We are going to gather here and pray till daybreak." If we will watch, the Lord will transform us as believers from a motley crew into ones who know authority before God—individually and corporately. The Lord transforms the church into His glorious bride and gives us a new name. This is a process, of course, of going from glory to glory, but God is actively changing us through the watch.

The Passover watch

During the first Passover, God moved to bring His people out of four hundred thirty years of bondage in Egypt through many unprecedented and unusual means. The Israelites, after slaying the Passover lamb, applied its blood to their houses and roasted and ate the lamb's flesh. They stayed awake through the night, not leaving their houses, and watched for the hand of the Lord to bring their deliverance. That night was to be commemorated from then on:

> Because the LORD kept vigil that night to bring them out of Egypt, on this night all the Israelites are to keep vigil to honor the LORD for the generations to come.
>
> —EXODUS 12:42, NIV

Today, God is calling His covenant people to the power of the Lamb and the night watch vigil once again.

The harlot Rahab

Rahab is also a picture for us of the watchman who lays hold of a fresh promise in the midst of devastation and the threat of destruction. She lived on the city wall, the place where watchmen kept their charge. On the basis of her faith in the God of Israel, she received the Lord's messengers, the men sent by Joshua to spy out Jericho. Rahab had heard of the God of Israel, and she believed. She didn't wait for disaster to come. She negotiated with the men of God beforehand, just as we seek God in the watch to avert trouble. Her intercession for her whole family—positioning herself in the breach where the trouble was to come and destroy her house—saved her whole family.

I've heard that archeologists studying the ruins of Jericho tell of one place in the wall that did not topple. We know that Rahab's house was on the wall: "For her house was on the city wall; she dwelt on the wall" (Josh. 2:15). Yet when the walls fell, Joshua sent men to Rahab's house to save her and her whole family, saying, "Go into the harlot's house, and from there bring out the woman and all that she has, as you swore to her" (Josh. 6:22). So, though the walls around the entire city fell down flat, the place where Rahab's house rested stayed standing!

Rahab gathered her whole family in her house—"her father, her mother, her brothers…all her relatives" (Josh. 6:23). They all came under her covering, under the contract she made with the men of God. Her faith won for her a place as the ancestor of King David and of the Messiah Himself. She truly was a watchman on the wall for her house.

The prophet Samuel

The prophet Samuel knew about communing with God at night. He received his first lesson as a child when God called to him. Samuel didn't know the voice of God yet, but Eli the priest, with whom the young Samuel was living in the temple, finally realized that it was God calling the little boy. He told Samuel to reply, "Speak, LORD, for Your servant hears," the next time he was called (1 Sam. 3:9). Samuel did that the next time he heard his name, and the Lord instructed him in the night hours.

Later, when God rejected Saul as king of Israel, Samuel was grieved. He "cried out to the LORD all night" (1 Sam. 15:11). Watching and praying were a continuing part of Samuel's relationship with the Lord.

King David

David seems to have spent many nights awake with the Lord, both as a shepherd and a king. When David and Bathsheba's son lay dying, David sought mercy from God; he "fasted and went in and lay all night on the ground" (2 Sam. 12:16).

We are also given a glimpse into David's deep relationship with God in the night hours in these verses from the Book of Psalms:

> I meditate on You in the night watches.
>
> —PSALM 63:6

> My heart also instructs me in the night seasons. I have set the LORD always before me.
>
> —PSALM 16:7–8

> O My God, I cry...in the night season, and am not silent.
>
> —PSALM 22:2

David was also a musician whose anointed music calmed King Saul when he was in a rage. Growing up as a shepherd, David no doubt spent many nights alone with the sheep, singing and playing new songs to the Lord. He was used to pouring out his heart to God at night in psalms and poems. David was a man truly "after [God's] own heart" (1 Sam. 13:14).

King Solomon

David's son Solomon received visits from God during the night, a time when God loves to speak to His people. The first night visit happened when Solomon, early in his reign, went to the tabernacle and sacrificed one thousand burnt offerings to the Lord.

> On that night God appeared to Solomon, and said to him, "Ask! What shall I give you?"
>
> —2 CHRONICLES 1:7

Now that is a question we all would like to hear from God. Solomon answered with humility, asking for wisdom to govern the people well, and God granted it.

Later, after the dedication of the new temple that Solomon built, "the LORD appeared to Solomon by night, and said to him: 'I have heard your prayer...'" (2 Chron. 7:12). It was at that time that God revealed that "if My people who are called by My name will humble themselves, and pray and seek My face, and turn from their wicked ways, then I will hear from heaven, and will forgive their sin and heal their land" (v. 14). Solomon bore much fruit from being alert to God's presence at night.

Daniel and the king

Every Sunday school child can tell you the story of Daniel in the lions' den. Did you ever think of that as a watch before the Lord? I'm quite sure that Daniel stayed awake and prayed while he was in that lions' den, aren't you?

King Darius as well "went to his palace and spent the night fasting; and no musicians were brought before him. Also his sleep went from him" (Dan. 6:18). The king cared for Daniel and wanted Daniel delivered from death. When he called to Daniel in the lions' den early the next morning, he acknowledged Daniel as "servant of the living God...whom you serve continually" (v. 20).

Watchman's Hall of Fame

We can create our own Watchman's Hall of Fame from the Old Testament, modeled after the Faith Hall of Fame in Hebrews 11. As the writer of Hebrews said, "Time would fail me to tell of..." all those who could be inducted (v. 32).

The prophet Habakkuk wrote, "I will stand my watch and set myself on the rampart, and watch to see what He will say to me" (Hab. 2:1). Ezekiel wrote, "I have made you a watchman for the house of Israel; therefore you shall hear a word from My mouth and warn them for Me" (Ezek. 33:7).

As we will learn, the Gentile Ruth watched all night at the feet of Boaz, and then she became his wife (Ruth 3). Nehemiah watched before and during the time he supervised the rebuilding of the walls of Jerusalem, as we will see (Neh. 4:6–14).

Throughout history, those who have apprehended the truth of what it means to watch and pray have been used by God to usher in a mighty move of His Spirit. One forceful example is Joel.

FROM DESOLATION TO RESTORATION

THE BOOK OF Joel begins with a terrifying picture of total destruction. Enemy troops have overrun the nation. Villages lie in ruin. Widows weep over Israel's slain defenders. The harvest smolders after being set ablaze by enemy torches. Young maidens, ravished by the marauders, cover their faces in shame. The land, once a Garden of Eden, is now a desolate wilderness.

The desolation has touched every aspect of the people's lives. There is no oil, no harvest, no feasting, no food. Even worship is interrupted, for there is no grain or wine for sacrifices. Joy is gone. The priests mourn. The land mourns.

The land needed rain—physical and spiritual rain. In the aftermath of this catastrophe, there was just one thing to do: Cry out to God! And so the call goes forth—a universal call that touches every home and every tribe.

> Blow the trumpet in Zion,
> Consecrate a fast,
> Call a sacred assembly;
> Gather the people,
> Sanctify the congregation,
> Assemble the elders,
> Gather the children and nursing babes;
> Let the bridegroom go out from his chamber,
> And the bride from her dressing room.
>
> —JOEL 2:15–16

> Come, lie all night...
>
> —JOEL 1:13

23

None were to be excluded. The people were to pray, weeping before God, pouring out their grief unto the Lord as they repented before Him and petitioned Him for intervention. Only the Lord in His great mercy could provide the hope they needed for the future.

The Book of Joel provides us with a picture of a nation called to repentance, called to stand in the gap between God and more desolation. We are called to do that today for America. "Turn to the Lord," the prophet exhorts. "Who knows if He will turn and relent, and leave a blessing behind Him?" (Joel 2:14).

God is indeed gracious and full of restoration, Joel tells the people:

> Rejoice, O sons of Zion, and be glad in the LORD your God; for He has given you the early rain for your vindication. And He has poured down for you the rain, the early and latter rain as before.
>
> And the threshing floors will be full of grain, and the vats will overflow with the new wine and oil. Then I will make up to you for the years that the swarming locust has eaten . . . and you shall have plenty to eat and be satisfied, and praise the name of the LORD your God, who has dealt wondrously with you.
>
> —JOEL 2:23–26, NAS

The watch in the Old Testament is a type of learning to rely on God and not on the arm of flesh. That is still a foundational truth for the New Testament watch. We watch because we are fully aware that, as Jesus said, "He who abides in Me, and I in him, bears much fruit; for without Me you can do nothing" (John 15:5). We need the intimacy, power and ability we receive as we spend time watching and praying with the Lord.

JESUS AND THE WATCH

BEFORE THE DAYS of Christ, people watched and prayed out of their desperate needs. But the times Jesus spent watching were more times of communing intimately with His Father. His times of watching were a source of life for Him, a relationship with Abba Father. And, of course, there He received the revelations and instructions He needed to fulfill His purpose on earth.

The anointing for miracles, signs and wonders always costs something. It's not just about lining up and having hands laid on for the impartation to move in the miraculous realm of the Spirit. There is a price to pay for anyone who wants that level of anointing. Part of the cost is to watch and pray. Then the power of God is released.

The power of God released

When Jesus was baptized by John, the Holy Spirit descended on Him like a dove (Luke 3:22). Then Jesus, filled with the Holy Spirit, was led by Him in to the wilderness to be tempted forty days by the devil. During that time He fasted and prayed (Luke 4:1–2). All of us know the story of the temptations He faced while there and how He stood against Satan's wiles. But do you know how He emerged from that time of fasting and prayer?

> Then Jesus returned in the *power* of the Spirit to Galilee, and news of Him went out through all the surrounding region.
> —LUKE 4:14, ITALICS ADDED

Jesus entered the wilderness *full* of the Holy Spirit, but He left in the *power* of the Holy Spirit. Suddenly, news went everywhere about Him. News spreads fast when God's power is manifesting.

A habit of watching

As we began to seek the Lord regarding how to usher in—and keep—the glory of God in our midst, we suddenly saw something critical to our understanding of the ministry of the miraculous: Keeping watch all night in prayer was one of the practical foundations of Jesus' earthly ministry. Preceding the miracles He did and His acts of healing and deliverance, there was one common thread: He stayed up all night and prayed. Jesus literally fasted sleep to pray—and the miracles followed.

> Now it came to pass in those days that He [Jesus] went out to
> the mountain to pray, and continued all night in prayer to God.
> And when it was day, He called His disciples to Himself; and
> from them He chose twelve whom He also named apostles.
> —LUKE 6:12–13

Two things happened when Jesus came down from praying all night on the mountain. First, Jesus received instructions on whom to select as apostles. He named those disciples "apostles" and released them into the apostolic anointing. He watched, then He released the apostles. From this, we see that the apostolic anointing will be released as we watch and pray.

Pastors and those of you who are hungry for the emerging of the apostolic church—the church full of signs and wonders—watch and pray! The New Testament church is an apostolic church with the apostolic anointing. One of the keys to releasing the apostolic anointing is watching and praying. It is more crucial to pray one hour than to teach ten hours on prayer.

I believe God in this hour is helping the church to transition into becoming an apostolic people. It's important to go from teaching about prayer to doing it. As Bonnie and I have experienced it, the river of watching and prayer is wonderful. People have been looking at the river, describing the river and taking all kinds of measurements of it. Believe us, the water is fine. Jump in!

The other thing that happened after Jesus spent the night awake, praying on that mountain, was that the multitudes came to hear Him, and they were blessed with a great outpouring of healing, deliverance and a release of the miraculous.

> And He came down [the mountain] with them [His newly
> selected apostles] and stood on a level place with a crowd of His
> disciples and a great multitude of people from all Judea and
> Jerusalem, and from the seacoast of Tyre and Sidon, who came
> to hear Him and be healed of their diseases, as well as those who
> were tormented with unclean spirits. And they were healed. And

the whole multitude sought to touch Him, for *power* went out
from Him and healed them all.

—Luke 6:17–19, italics added

Power comes with a price. But let me tell you, the price pales in comparison to the miracles, the healings and the intimacy with God.

The Garden of Gethsemane

Jesus was in the process of watching in the Garden of
Gethsemane when the Roman centurions came to arrest Him on the
night He was betrayed. It was so common for Him to go to this
place that Judas knew exactly where to find Him: "He went to the
Mount of Olives as He was accustomed, and His disciples also followed Him" (Luke 22:39). He prayed there often.

This is the ultimate example of the kind of watch about which Joel
spoke. Jesus Himself became the land in utter destruction, totally
cut off from God. He was about to make intercession with His own
body. So He kept a watch in relation to becoming the ultimate intercessor—placing His body between God and man.

So Jesus watched the night before His betrayal. Out of this
lifestyle of prayer He asked Peter at Gethsemane, "Could you not
watch with Me one hour?" (Matt. 26:40). Jesus even told them the
value of watching: "Watch and pray, lest you enter into temptation.
The spirit indeed is willing, but the flesh is weak" (v. 41). Watching
would give them the power they would need in the hour that was
coming upon them. Yet Jesus knew that the flesh fought this, so He
encouraged them all the more.

"I say to all: Watch!"

Before He went to the cross the disciples asked Jesus for the signs of
His coming and the end of the age. Jesus told them of different signs,
but then He gave them the prescription for preparing for His coming:
"What I say to you, I say to all: Watch!" (Mark 13:37). All means *all!*

The Greek word for "watch" that Jesus used, *gregoreuo,* means
"be vigilant, wake, (be) watch(ful)." Luke 21:36 reiterates this plea:

"Watch therefore, and pray always." The Greek word used here is *agrupneo*, which means "to be sleepless, keep awake...watch."

Jesus was telling the End-Time church that one of the primary ways to prepare for the Bridegroom coming back is for the church to watch and pray. And He spoke to *all*. That means everybody. This is the scriptural command of the Lord Himself to all believers—not to just a few leaders, and not to just a few who "feel called" to intercession.

If watching and praying were necessary for Jesus to receive power to minister, then these disciplines may also be necessary for us. Do you want to move in the power and anointing of God? Do you want miracles? Do you want to see the End-Time harvest and the glorious return of the Lord? This is part of the prescription. There is never a substitute for spending that quality time in prayer with the Father. It behooves us to do that individually as well as corporately.

WATCHES IN THE NEW TESTAMENT

JESUS SET THE pattern for the new kind of watch—one of intimacy and power. Many people followed His example.

The widow Anna

The prophetess Anna, a widow from her young years, came continually to the temple to minister to the Lord. She was about eighty-four, but the Bible records that she "served God with fastings and prayers night and day" (Luke 2:37). Because of her intimacy with God, Anna knew that the baby Jesus brought into the temple by Mary and Joseph was the Messiah. Perhaps her intercession played a key role in bringing forth the Messiah.

In one accord

After Jesus' ascension to heaven, we see the apostles and the followers of Christ always together praying:

They all joined together constantly in prayer, along with the women and Mary, the mother of Jesus, and with his brothers.

—ACTS 1:14, NIV

Ten days after the ascension, they were still watching and praying:

When the Day of Pentecost had fully come, they were all with one accord in one place.

—ACTS 2:1

At that time, the Holy Spirit came upon them suddenly, and they were all filled with the Holy Spirit and spoke with other tongues. Here we see the power of corporate prayer and unity. Corporate prayer without unity is powerless.

The free church keeps watch.

Some time later, when the new church had been scattered by persecution, Peter was arrested by King Herod and put into prison. He was bound with two chains and was ordered to be guarded by four squads of four soldiers each. He slept between two soldiers, and sentries stood guard at the cell entrance.

But the power of man is nothing in relation to the power of God. "So Peter was kept in prison, but the church was earnestly praying to God for him" (Acts 12:5, NIV). The church was keeping watch.

The night before Herod wanted to bring Peter to trial, an angel came to Peter and woke him up. His chains fell off, and the angel led Peter past all the guards and out of the prison. At first Peter thought he was having a vision, but when he found himself in the street, the truth dawned on him: "Now I know without a doubt that the Lord sent his angel and rescued me from Herod's clutches and from everything the Jewish people were anticipating" (v. 11, NIV).

Peter made his way to the house of Mary, the mother of Mark, "where many people had gathered and were praying" (v. 12, NIV). At first, the "believers" didn't believe the servant girl Rhoda when she told them that Peter was at the door. Then Peter came in and related what had happened, and they were all astonished.

Here we see the church, out of their concern for the one in chains, watching and praying, and Peter is released. Watching in corporate prayer is the genetic code of the apostolic church.

The church in chains keeps watch.

When Paul and Silas were in Philippi, they were followed by a slave girl who had a spirit that allowed her to make money for her owners by fortunetelling. Paul cast the spirit out of her, which greatly upset her owners, who now were unable to make money with her. They seized Paul and Silas and took them before the magistrates. There the crowd joined in the attack, and the magistrates ordered Paul and Silas to be beaten severely and kept in the inner prison.

When you visit places like the prisons the Romans used, you see that this innermost dungeon is a terrible place to be—full of raw sewage, rats and roaches. Plus, the jailer had fastened their feet in stocks, and they were in great agony. They had been flogged severely, they were bruised and bloody, yet what were they doing?

"About midnight Paul and Silas were praying and singing hymns to God, and the other prisoners were listening to them" (Acts 16:25, NIV). They were having a watch of their own, down in the deepest dungeon where no light could enter.

"Suddenly there was a great earthquake, so that the foundations of the prison were shaken; and immediately all the doors were open and everyone's chains were loosed" (v. 26). They were watching at midnight, and the miracle came.

The jailer was about to kill himself because he thought everyone had escaped. Paul called out to him not to harm himself. When this happened, the jailer knew to whom to give the credit. He called for lights and fell down before Paul and Silas, asking, "What must I do to be saved?" (v. 30). And he was saved, along with his household.

Here God is showing us the power of the watch. It's not just your chains that are loosed, your door that is opened. The doors of the entire prison were opened; the chains of every prisoner were loosed. That is the glory of the power of watching. We can supernaturally break the chains—broken homes, addictions, oppressions—covering multitudes of people with prayer and watching. As you pray for your children, your sons and daughters, your brothers and sisters, your mothers and fathers, your neighbors—their chains will fall off.

Here the church in chains is the intercessor. The Lord visits them, and everyone is released.

The apostolic ministry and the watch

Paul is commending his apostolic ministry in 2 Corinthians 6: "In stripes, in imprisonments, in tumults, in labours, in watchings, in fastings . . ." (v. 5, KJV). Again, in chapter 11 he says, "In weariness and painfulness, in watchings often, in hunger and thirst, in fastings often, in cold and nakedness" (v. 27, KJV). Paul knew that watching and prayer were part of the apostolic ministry, the New Testment church. He was willing to pay the price.

Later Paul said, "I have fought the good fight, I have finished the race, I have kept the faith. Finally, there is laid up for me the crown of righteousness" (2 Tim. 4:7–8). He knew that it was a fight, but he knew it was worth it.

A Secret History With God

PRAYER IS WHERE everything begins and ends in the spirit, where everything is accomplished. I've heard people say that they are called to preach, to lay hands on the sick, to evangelize, but not to intercede. The truth is that we should not be ministering to others if we have not spent time communing with and receiving from the One who ordains the anointing for all ministry. The miracles of Jesus' ministry came out of His watch nights with God.

As believers, we must have a hidden place in the Lord to have a public place in the Lord. A secret place gives you a reward openly. You must have a secret history with the Lord. No secret history, no public miracles. People want to come into the greater works, but they don't want to come into the secret history.

If we will grasp this, we will covet our personal time with God. It is a key to the anointing and victory in God. Most of the time, we see the things about people that are public. But if we miss out on the secret part, if we let it get weak, then the public part will falter. This is true of individuals and churches, too. Pastors need to be very wise, ensuring that they and their people are maintaining their secret places before the Lord. This must be guarded and cherished. If we are missing out on the private time, then it will eventually show up in public.

"All my springs are in you" (Ps. 87:7). We may see the river out there in public, but the river originates from an underground spring. We must take care of that spring.

Jesus had the habit of going off to pray. If not daily, it was at least several times a week. He watched all night and ministered during the day. This was His hidden life, His secret life with God.

TEACH US TO PRAY

THE DISCIPLES CAME to Jesus and said, "Lord, teach us to pray" (Luke 11:1). They didn't say, "Teach us how to make disciples. Teach us how to build a big church. Teach us the precepts of the Law as You understand them." They said, "Teach us to pray."

I believe those men who knew the Lord best knew this about Him: He was first and foremost a man of communion with God, a man of prayer. Jesus' example of prayer no doubt prompted the disciples' desire to learn how to pray as He did. They saw the power that prayer released in His life, and they coveted the kind of relationship Jesus had with the Father. They made the connection that His time with the Father was the key.

From these and other examples, we see that through watching, God brings solutions into being. Through watching, we get to know God. We can be filled with His anointing and His power to do great exploits in His name.

Since Jesus watched all night in prayer, we can expect to reap powerful results in the realm of the Spirit if we follow that same pattern. Now, I would like to show you the pattern God has given us for our watches.

32

And what I say to you, I say to all: Watch!

—MARK 13:37

3

The Watch of the Lord

---

§

"PRAY ALL NIGHT?" you will probably ask. "How can anyone pray all night?"

It's easy. Bonnie and I discovered long ago, during the foundational days of our global prayer and healing ministry, that while prayer is the calling of God to all believers, it is our decision whether we respond or not. Once we make the commitment to seek God's face in prayer, He honors our decision by empowering us with a special outpouring of His grace, strength and physical stamina.

Prayer has always been a foundation of our ministry. Ever since the beginning, the Lord has impressed upon me the necessity to fast and pray on a regular basis. As a result I have witnessed God's miracle-working power operate in many nations. I have watched as masses of people were touched by God's healing power. I have seen God move against the powers of witchcraft and demonic forces, breaking their power and setting the oppressed free. On one occasion, I saw a child raised from the dead. The secret to this ministry has always been the anointing of God that is released through prayer and fasting.

Prayer, to Bonnie and me, has never been a duty. It is our precious privilege to walk into the throne room of the King of kings and gain an audience with Him. He always gives gifts to His guests. He never sends us away empty.

THE DESIGN OF THE WATCH

FOR EIGHT HOURS each Friday night, we come before the Lord, fasting from food and sleep, in order to focus on vital issues to attack in prayer that the Holy Spirit reveals to us. Corporately, the body of Christ has not done much praying at night. But the Lord often visits at night, as we saw in Scripture and as Bonnie and I have seen in our lives.

The thief also comes at night. So we must mount an offensive attack at night, encroaching on the enemy's territory. Why is this so significant? Because the enemy of our souls is busiest at night, while most of us are sleeping. It is the night—the darkness—that has previously been Satan's prized possession. Through the Watch of the Lord, we are taking back the night and claiming it on behalf of its Creator, the Lord Most High.

The watch starts at 10 P.M. and ends at 6 A.M. In order to prepare for the watch, we do take little catnaps if we can fit them in during the day on Friday. We also try to keep a lighter schedule that day. Our family sits down to dinner at least an hour earlier than usual. If our ministry schedule permits, we then rest until it is time to head for church.

We fast from chitchat and socializing at the watch in order to give the Lord and His purposes our full attention. Those who come to pray with us during the Watch of the Lord are free to leave early if they must. They are also free to nap awhile if necessary in order to complete the last few hours of the watch.

We always wait on the Lord to determine His agenda. We praise and worship first for a long time, using two worship teams so they don't get weary. Then praise and worship is interspersed throughout the night.

Ministry usually begins around midnight, when we enter into corporate intercession for global ministries and for the nations. At one point we bring the American flag and the Israeli flag out to the center in front of the stage. Watchmen come and lay hands on the flags, and we pray for a concentrated time for God's land, Israel, and the nation in which we live. We pray for America, her leaders and the concerns reflected in the day's headlines. We pray for the leaders of the world, sometimes bringing out a world map, and for God's will to be established throughout the earth.

The Holy Spirit quickens various scriptures to us throughout the course of the watch. We receive a living word from God each week—the essence of what He appears to be saying to His corporate body at that given time. This word guides us as a group through the week to come and reveals through Scripture and prophetic words a useful strategy that helps us navigate our way.

We sing, dance, clap and enjoy being together as we pray and intercede. Prayer requests we've received are passed out and prayed over. We also are careful to pray for our staff, other ministries, our police force, the schools and other agencies. We always celebrate communion, usually toward the end of the watch.

Often the gifts of the Spirit flow, and we lose all track of time as the Holy Spirit moves in our midst, performing healings, releasing prophecy and touching His people in His deep and profound way. Always we take our direction from the Lord, for He is Captain of the watch.

A normal watch may find prayer warriors at the altar, some fallen out around the altar under the power of God as they "soak" in His presence and some dotted throughout the auditorium curled up in sleeping bags or with blankets and pillows. We are very informal during these all-night prayer vigils.

Week to week, our prayer focus is always the higher agenda of the kingdom of God, rather than our own personal needs fulfilled. After we have focused on and prayed for the things on God's heart, the

Holy Spirit will normally minister to our personal needs. We often have a time of personal ministry around 5 A.M., but that is not our primary purpose in coming together. Bonnie and I have discovered that when we seek first the kingdom of God, our personal needs are met supernaturally! It is just as Jesus said: "Seek ye first the kingdom of God, and his righteousness; and all these things shall be added unto you" (Matt. 6:33, KJV).

THE FOURTH WATCH OF THE NIGHT

THE GLORY OF God seems to increase in our midst as we continue to watch and pray. During the fourth watch (between 3 A.M. and 6 A.M.), it is multiplied and the miracles begin. It was during the fourth watch of the night that Jesus walked on the water out to His disciples who were in a boat on the lake, striving against the storm (Mark 6:48).

In our watch, there is a special excitement and an open heaven in the hours just before the light. When we are at our weakest physically, the Holy Spirit comes in His greatest strength with prayer, revelation and refreshing. A lot of the miracles, healing and specific supernatural intelligence we receive is during this time, even though it is the time when the fewest people are present.

During a military campaign, the hours of the fourth watch are the most strategic hours of the night, the most difficult time frame wherein to guard against the enemy's attack and the time the enemy is most likely to attack. During times of war, about half an hour before both sunrise and sunset, a stand-to is conducted in the military. That means everyone is alert, packed up and ready to fight or move at a moment's notice. This is when the enemy is likely to attack.

Medical personnel have another term for it—the *dead of night,* the time span when more deaths occur than any other segment of our twenty-four-hour day. Biblically speaking, it's the time when the enemy of our souls is busiest, when soldiers watch most earnestly and when we must watch for God's instructions as we stand our posts on the wall of prayer.

When Gideon sought to build an army to deliver Israel from the Midianites, only three hundred out of thirty-two thousand were fit to go to war. God had Gideon choose the men who remained watchful, vigilant and alert, even when they were faced with a powerful physical need—quenching their thirst. The men God chose for Gideon were always on the alert. They epitomized the military rigor of the watch, or keeping vigil.

When we worship, war and watch, the glory comes. And when the glory comes, there is great grace for healing, ministry, miracles and the prophetic. When the presence of the Lord comes, there is clarity of vision. Watchmen are able to be first partakers of that clarity since they are watching from the lookout posts on the wall. They have a greater vantage point in the realm of the spirit, so they can see what's coming and warn the rest of the body of Christ of any trouble or turbulence ahead.

IN HIS PRESENCE

EVEN EIGHT HOURS of intense, concentrated, corporate prayer really do pass quickly. We literally lose all track of time as we are caught up in the presence of the Lord. The power of God is demonstrated again and again, and all too soon, it's over—until the following week when we gather again to watch on the wall in prayer.

People ask me, "Pastor, what if I get sleepy?" My answer is, "Sleep!" People bring their sleeping bags, blankets and pillows. Watching is like exercising a new muscle. So we encourage people not to stay away because they know they will fall asleep. Get in His presence. Be there as His visitation comes.

Remember Aaron's rod: It sprouted and blossomed while it lay in the tent of meeting. The rod wasn't praying or asking to grow; it was a dead stick. But it was in the presence of God, and the anointing changed the rod. So we tell people—and their children—to come and sleep when they need to. We can absorb the glory of God, sleeping or awake—our children, too. They will remember, "My fanatic parents used to watch all night, and I would lie on the rug and sleep."

This is liberty, not legalism. As Jesus said, "Beware of the leaven of the Pharisees" (Luke 12:1).

I will admit that at the end, we're a little punchy from the lack of sleep. But at the same time we feel great. We have found that the Lord uses even a little nap the next day to refresh those who watch with Him. He makes it up to us.

CHILDREN IN THE WATCH

"LET THE LITTLE children come to Me, and do not forbid them; for of such is the kingdom of God" (Mark 10:14). From the beginning of the watch we have delighted in having children participate. They are involved actively in the worship, ministry and exercise of prophetic gifts.

The little ones look forward to watch night services because they can worship and be near their friends. I see the principle of spiritual osmosis at work with many of the babies and toddlers. They seem to "absorb" the atmosphere of praise and worship.

For the older children, the watch has been instrumental in stirring their hearts of devotion to the Lord and has given them the confidence to move in spiritual gifts, including prophecy. A young lady named Gillian has spent the last several years growing into her teens, being a faithful watchman. Her prophetic anointing keeps growing stronger. At the age of twelve she shared this word in the watch: "I had a vision of credits rolling at the end of a movie. I felt that God was saying, 'Don't think that what you do for the kingdom goes unnoticed, no matter how small it is. On judgment day God will roll the credits of the movie of life and every good work will be rewarded.'"

Faith, a faithful teen watchman from South Carolina, wrote this poem concerning the watch:

Watching, sighting
Waiting, fighting,
Dusk till dawn,

40

While children yawn,
Still we all are pressing on.

No eat, no sleep,
One face we seek,
The face of One,
God's only Son.

Interceding,
By the Spirit's leading.
Sword and shield,
People healed.

Trumpets sound,
Holy ground,
Angels near,
Do not fear.

Tearing down,
Walls all around.
Enemies routed,
As we shouted.
Demons flee,
Captives set free.

THE TENT OF PRAYER

DO YOU WANT God's address? Do you want to know where His house is? His address is prayer. "My house shall be called a house of prayer" (Matt. 21:13). When Jesus went into the temple with all the buying, selling, conversing and taking care of business, He took one look and said, "I don't live here." He declared that His house would be "a house of prayer for all nations" (Mark 11:17). Jesus didn't say the church would be a house of doctrine or teaching or a house of wisdom or prophecy. He didn't even say it was going to be a house of miracles! He said first and foremost, "My house will be a house of prayer."

For our purposes, we define prayer as communion with God. For us, prayer is like a large tent that holds under it other aspects of communion with Him. Many people still think of prayer as sitting down with a little list of things to ask God to do. But prayer is really drawing near to God and being with Him.

As we pray together corporately, seven things combine into a wonderful mix that, when led by the Holy Spirit, creates an atmosphere conducive to the presence of God.

- Praise
- Worship
- Thanksgiving
- Supplication
- Intercession
- Prophecy
- Proclamation

Week to week, each of these seven elements seems to be present to some degree. But it's not as if we deliberately try to attend to all of these priorities during any given watch. We simply exalt Jesus, love Him and worship at His feet; only in looking back do we discover that we have spent time on each of these aspects of prayer. We also do some preaching, although we devote the least attention to preaching in order to keep the focus on prayer.

THE WATCH: A FRIEND TO THE PASTOR

PASTORS, IF YOU let a watch happen in your church on Friday night—or any night—you will find so much oil of the Holy Spirit in your church that preaching on Sunday morning will never be a problem. You will not have to "pray through" because the whole place will be soaking in the oil of the Holy Spirit. The servants of God who are to minister on Sunday will just wallow in the river with joy. Our experience is that God's presence will be there.

As a practical discipling tool, the watch is a great friend to the local pastor. As the people come and submit to the corporate watch experience, they find themselves on God's threshing floor where the grain is winnowed.

The winnowing process involves separating grain from the chaff, which is the outer covering of the grain. In Bible times, the grain was often tread by oxen, then tossed into the air so the breeze could blow away the chaff. Barley is a type or a symbol for humanity; our frames are like grass. In His presence, Bonnie and I have experienced the removal of chaff from our lives by His blowing on us with the wind of the Holy Spirit.

This is wonderful for a pastor; he doesn't have to labor over all the specific points of chaff in people's lives. If they can consistently get into the river of the Holy Spirit at the watch, the Lord Himself will do the changing. The Lord is there.

This threshing begins to loosen up strongholds in the souls of those who are watching, because as they are communing with Jesus, they are being changed. As Jesus prayed, He "was transfigured" (Matt. 17:2, KJV). As the church prays, she is transfigured and changed, and the bride is revealed. We are being transformed from glory to glory.

We have noticed that the watchmen who come faithfully are changed. Something happens to them: The flightiness and immaturity go away; so does the disappointment when God does not move immediately on some issue. Instead, they learn about the triumph that comes with standing through anything.

A watchman from Kentucky writes about the personal changes she's had from watching: "I have experienced new intimacy with the Lord. He has started to deal with me about some of my religiosity and judgmental attitudes, and I believe I'm not as self-centered as I was six months ago. He's given me a new desire to reach the lost, and I love Him more than ever. He's my best Friend and constant Companion."

A watchman from Indiana draws this conclusion: "As we look at the people who have been consistently involved in the watch, especially at ourselves, we see a major heart change. Our intimacy with the Lord is at a new level, especially in worship and praise. We only desire more of Him. Also, He has imparted to us a heart for the lost that we never had before. We cry out for Israel and the nations as we never were able to do before. We see a breaking down of walls between denominations and a love for our brothers and sisters in the Lord. He is giving us a desire to know the love of the Father more and more and then extend that love to others."

When these changes occur in people, pastors don't have to spend all those hours in counseling. I used to spend hours in counseling; now I spend maybe an hour a week.

For pastors who want the apostolic released, let people hold watches in your churches. On Sunday mornings the signs and wonders will start taking place, and the prophetic will flow in such a beautiful way. Because of the watching and praying, the healing river comes. I challenge pastors to start doing this and see if it doesn't change the atmosphere on Sunday morning, as well as bring the spirit of revival and healing.

THE REWARDS OF THE WATCH

EVER SINCE WE first heard God's call to corporate prayer, we have faithfully set aside one night each week to watch all night and pray. As I said earlier, it is a sweet privilege to spend this time with the Lord. After a watch, Bonnie says she feels as if she has been washed with rain. He always deposits a treasure in our hearts. We never leave unfulfilled.

Bonnie and I have come to realize that there are many advantages to seeking God's kingdom first. Because we made ourselves available, miracles began to happen. Healings are not uncommon. Dreams and visions have increased. Every week we receive testimonies of dreams and visions other watchmen have received in watches all over the country and the world.

For instance, from one watch in Ontario, Canada, we received the word that as they prayed, one watchman saw a fellow watchman with bronze boxing gloves on. With her worship, she was punching holes in the sky, making the way to God clear—and the enemy hated it. Another watchman received a vision of a heart that was enlarging and growing until it encompassed all of the United States. She sensed that the task of the harvest was not too large when seen from God's perspective, that all the nations are on the Lord's heart and encompassed by His heart.

Also, ever since we said, "OK, we'll watch," we have entered into a flow of the Holy Spirit in which His will just seems to be done. His mind is revealed to us. Doors open to us supernaturally, and divine connections are set across our paths.

Over and above that, the Lord has allowed us to enter into Sabbath rest that is very supernatural. The best part is the peace of God—His *shalom*—that has settled upon our household and our ministry as a result of our commitment to pray faithfully all night each Friday and to diligently watch at the wall. This peace of God, the peace that passes all understanding, appears to be a by-product of first taking care of God's priorities; it is not something for which we had to work in order to obtain. We have labored to enter into His rest, and the peace is His reward.

The rewards of keeping the watch are consistent with the rewards of fasting. We fast our sleep; we fast our food; we fast from our own agendas; we fast from doing our own desires during the watch time. Isaiah 58 lists the rewards of the fast God acknowledges:

- The bonds of wickedness will be cut (v. 6).
- The oppressed will go free (v. 6).
- The yokes of oppression will be broken (v. 6).
- Your light shall break forth like a daily sunrise (v. 8).
- Healing will come speedily (v. 8).
- Your righteousness will be your reputation preceding you (v. 8).
- The glory of the Lord shall follow and guard you (v. 8).
- Your prayer will be answered immediately (v. 9).
- The Lord will manifest Himself in your midst (v. 9).

- Your light will shine in the midst of darkness (v. 10).
- Your darkest times will still be like noonday sun (v. 10).
- You will have continual guidance from the Lord (v. 11).
- You will be full in time of leanness (v. 11).
- You will be filled with strength in the very center of your life (v. 11).
- The Holy Spirit will water you and make you fruitful and beautiful (v. 11).
- The Holy Spirit will fill you daily and make you like a spring that never runs dry (v. 11).
- You will be a repairer of the breach, a restorer of streets in which to dwell (v. 12).
- You will be delighted with God (v. 14).
- You will have authority with those in authority and have power in difficult times (v. 14).

ANSWERED PRAYER

OF COURSE, SOME of the greatest rewards of the watch are answered prayers. "He who goes forth bearing seed and weeping [at needing his precious supply or grain for sowing], shall doubtless come again with rejoicing, bringing his sheaves with him" (Ps. 126:6, AMP). This has been the corporate and individual experience of the watchmen who have faithfully kept the watch. As we carry the burden of the Lord in our hearts, standing in the gap for the earth, the anointing accomplishes the will of God while the watchman carries away the spoils!

During one of our Friday night watches in Charlotte, we were intensely urged by the Holy Spirit to intercede specifically for the safety of our children. The next evening one of the couples who had been at the watch received a call that their daughter, who was visiting a friend in Colorado, had been thrown from a horse. Her foot became stuck in a stirrup, and she was dragged around the corral and struck her head on a rock. The physician examining her said she lost the vision in her left eye and was suffering from temporary amnesia due to a concussion.

This couple continued to trust God for their daughter's healing, mobilizing additional prayer support as CAT scans and further tests were ordered. A call from the physician the following day indicated great surprise on his part. "The eye that I examined immediately following the accident does not appear to be the same eye that I am now observing," he said. The physician, a born-again Christian, continued, "Your daughter has been miraculously touched by God! Her vision is restored."

There is no price that can be placed on an answered prayer like that.

We have also seen our prayers answered on a global scale. During April 1999 we were praying for the three American prisoners of the war with Yugoslavia to be released. On Friday night, April 30, we again held them up in prayer, specifically by name. We asked the Lord to cause Yugoslav President Milosevic to release them from prison.

During that same day, Friday, President Milosevic had said no to an interfaith delegation of American religious leaders negotiating in Belgrade for the soldiers' release. On Saturday, May 1, after our watch, President Milosevic did a complete turnaround and agreed to release the soldiers!

We are thrilled to have joined with other intercessors around the country, and perhaps the world, who were praying for their release.

THE WATCH OF THE LORD GROWS

THE WATCH DRAWS those from far and near. Bonnie and I are never quite sure whom we'll find there to pray with us as we show up. There may be fifty, one hundred fifty or as many as five hundred people. Invariably, some will have traveled great distances in order to watch with us. People from England, Australia, Brazil, Canada, Germany, Egypt, India, Bahrain and all parts of the United States have made the trip to sit up with us all night and pray.

Why in the world would anyone do that? Just to spend time with Bonnie and me and our ministry team? No. Word gets around that a very important Guest is with us weekly. His name is Jesus, and when He shows up, the miracles begin to flow. People have heard of the miraculous answers to prayer that have resulted from these all-night prayer meetings that take place in Charlotte, North Carolina, and those who have desperate need of a touch from the Lord just show up. And when the time is right, we pray for them.

Bonnie and I have also visited other churches and helped lead people in watches in different cities and nations. In Toronto, we led a watch where there were four thousand watchmen, and at 6:30 A.M., we served communion to twenty-five hundred. In Dallas, fifteen hundred kept the watch. Hundreds were in the watches we led in Sunderland and Bornemouth in England.

One thousand watched at a conference at Harvest Rock Church in Pasadena, California. On Friday night as I led the watch, I prayed to bind a spirit of witchcraft that had been oppressing and resisting those present by discouraging and draining them, rendering them ineffective in the anointing. As I prayed and broke the spiritual power of that spirit, outside the sanctuary on that clear night, the big tree that stands in the church entrance parking area split. Some people claim they heard the crack of a lightning bolt. The tree, minus a half, still stands there today as a reminder to those who know this story of the Lord who watches over His church to deliver us from the hand of the oppressor!

And, to my great joy, I have led hundreds in all-night prayer watches at the Western Wall in Jerusalem.

Our all-night prayer meetings that began in Charlotte are now being held in various cities in other nations. We communicate what God is saying to one another via telephone, mail, fax and the Internet. Prayer warriors from all parts of the globe join us as we cry out to God for just such an outpouring of His Spirit.

ANSWERING THE CALL

WHEN BONNIE OR I mention the Watch of the Lord in our travels, we don't have to use any selling tactics in order to get people involved in starting watches in their own communities. Everywhere we are met with the same response: "Yes! This is what we need! This is what we've been looking for!"

I can sense when others are vibrating to the same heavenly frequency as Bonnie and I are. It's as though these individuals are hearing a trumpet call—a supernatural sound from heaven calling them to the Watch of the Lord.

A GLOBAL VISION

WE HAVE A global vision, just as Jesus does. Bonnie received this vision about intercessors and the watch in 1986 during a personal time of watching in the night:

> I found myself in the midst of a vast unsettled territory like the high plains of the Midwest in America's pioneer history. The plain seemed deserted; only a strong wind (the Holy Spirit) was present. Suddenly through the tall golden grass I saw the top of a huge covered wagon slowly moving in the same direction as the wind. I was raised up so I could see the whole wagon. Stretched out before it was a team of eighteen to twenty sleek, muscular red-brown, long-horned oxen.
>
> I noticed several attributes the oxen had, including their disciplined harmony. They represented corporate prayer warriors, straining forward in unison. At the end of the day when they were unharnessed, they stood observing the busyness and laughter of the camp around them. They were patient, but each one anticipated being yoked up again to resume its task, as if they understood the importance of bringing their wagon to its destination.
>
> Then I noticed the Wagon Master, Jesus. He expressed a deep appreciation and affinity for these oxen. He made it very clear that in them was the sum of His wealth and His power to tame that wilderness. He loved the presence of the oxen because without them, He would be sitting alone atop that

wagon seat with all His precious cargo, without the force to carry the wagon forward.

I looked back over the prairie and noticed many teams with wagons crossing in every direction, each moving steadily toward their goal. As they heaved forward in the great wind, the same Wagon Master was seated on every wagon seat.

The Wagon Master pulled back the canvas of the wagon nearest us and showed me what was inside. "In here," He said, "are all the things that pertain to My kingdom being established on the earth." The wagon bed was filled with lots of tightly packed parcels representing all of God's will for mankind and for the earth literally wrapped in prayer. Now I understood why the Wagon Master so cherished these oxen. Without them, His precious cargo would never reach its destination.

Every one of those wagon teams were like little watches of people who were harmonizing together to bring the purposes of the Lord to their houses, their churches, their cities.

The final picture I saw was of the wagon tracks that had been cut through that prairie grass long after the wagons had passed over it. The Lord said, "Whether it be hours, days, weeks, months or years later, these tracks will be followed by those who will establish My kingdom and settle the things that these oxen, prayer warriors, have pulled through in prayer."

God is seeking people who will present themselves as living sacrifices—as oxen—and lay down their lives for prayer, fasting, watching and intercession. As we take prayer more to heart than ever before and commit to pray in a corporate manner, we will usher in this revival that will spread out from our cities into the nations, maybe leading to restoration and perhaps even reformation. Sustained, consistent, concerted, corporate, concentrated prayer will lead to sustained, glorious, spreading, strong, citywide, nationwide, worldwide revival. The revival will take place in our personal lives as well as in the church, once we learn how to vibrate according to the glory of the Lord.

When we learn how to bring down His presence, then sustain it, things will happen globally that you and I cannot even comprehend. That's what Bonnie and I are committed to seeing on earth today.

Our vision for the Watch of the Lord is bigger than a simple all-night prayer meeting in Charlotte, North Carolina. Our vision is as big as the world. It's not a heavy yoke. It's not a "have to," it's a "get to." It's a thrilling experience to be watchmen on the wall of prayer.

PART II

§

Be not ye afraid of them:
remember the Lord, which is great
and terrible, and fight for your brethren,
your sons, and your daughters, your wives,
and your houses.

—NEHEMIAH 4:14, KJV

4

The Wall of Prayer

§

THE LORD HAS confirmed to us that corporate prayer is His desire for us in this hour. One confirmation took place in the form of a vision that Bonnie had in January 1996.

I had gone on a personal retreat at Moravian Falls, North Carolina, for a week of prayer and fasting. On about the third or fourth day I was walking on a ridge and praying. The day was crisp and brightened by sunlight, and the natural setting made me feel enveloped in the beauty of God's creation.

As I was enjoying the beautiful panorama, I turned my head and saw a stone wall suddenly appear before me. The wall seemed to stretch forever, and in my spirit I knew that this wall stretched around the world.

The vision was so real, I felt as if I could reach my hand out and feel the sun-warmed stones. I walked along the base of the wall and in a moment came to a large breach in it. Time and the elements had broken down the wall there. Loose stones, eroding mortar and other debris were strewn in the opening.

As I looked through the breach I saw lands and nations. In the distance an enemy army was approaching—one that looked like the army of Kublai Khan. This army was mounted on horses and running pell-mell, covering as much land as possible in order to get through the breach in the wall. It was only a matter of time before this army of darkness would be upon the breach; its intent was to come through the wall before it was closed up and rendered impenetrable.

Just then I heard the voice of the Lord saying, "This is the wall of prayer. Corporate prayer will repair the breach." I turned and looked down the mountain and saw that this wall stretched below through city after city across nations and spanning seas. "I am calling workmen warriors back to this wall. You must repair the breaches."

The Lord spoke to my spirit as the vision continued: "This work of prayer is not a new work; it is an ancient one. You aren't building this wall. You are simply reinhabiting an old work." He spoke to me about the Moravians and their hundred-year revival.

Then the Lord said, "Just as the Great Wall of China is the only man-made structure on earth that can be seen from the heavens, so the work of prayer is the only work of man on earth that always has My attention from heaven. Rebuild the wall!"

The Lord caused me to understand that He wanted to close the breaches by stationing watchmen on the wall at strategic locations to repair the wall of prayer, to defend their families, cities and nations against the advancing invasion of Satan's dark armies. He was calling intercessors to set about the work of rebuilding the wall of prayer where prayer had ceased, from city to city, state to state and nation to nation, in order to ward off the armies of invaders—both our spiritual enemies and natural difficulties, such as disease, disasters, financial problems and the circumstances of life that tend to wear us down.

Those who hear and heed this call are commissioned to work rebuilding the wall through prayer and intercession. Our work is to rebuild that which has been torn down and trampled and to restore that which has been burned and left behind as worthless. The poor condition of the wall of prayer is the result of many generations of general prayerlessness and the practice of religious traditions without heartfelt relationship with the Lord.

HISTORY BEARS PROOF

IT IS SIGNIFICANT in many ways that Bonnie's vision occurred at Moravian Falls, the beautiful nature retreat named for the Moravians of the eighteenth century, who sparked a prayer and missions revival that lasted a hundred years. The Moravian Revival began in 1727 with the prayers of just one man—Count Nicholas von Zinzendorf.

THE HUNDRED-YEAR OUTPOURING

TOUCHED OFF BY the spiritual journey of Count Zinzendorf, the Moravians gathered at the count's castle, Herrnhut, which means "the Lord's watch," for a prayer meeting. Eventually joined by others—never more than three hundred at any given time—the Count established a twenty-four-hour prayer watch that stayed active for one hundred years. It was through the spiritual seeking of the Moravians that a significant portion of the developing world was evangelized during the last two centuries.

The Moravians' motto was a simple one, and it worked: "One at home, one in the field." The one at home was assigned the task of watching and praying. In so doing, the one in the field was covered and empowered by God to face any obstacle that might be placed in the way of the gospel. The Moravian Revival paved the way for the first modern missionaries to take the gospel around the world.

REVIVALS BIRTHED THROUGH PRAYER

EVEN THE WESLEY brothers were impacted by the Moravians, for it was through the Moravians that John Wesley first learned about the power of the Holy Spirit and that it did not pass away with the deaths of the twelve apostles. John Wesley, founder of the Methodists, understood the power of corporate prayer, as well as the importance of watching through the night in prayer. This is evidenced in his journal. An excerpt from 1739 reads:

> Mr. Hall, Kitchen, Ingam, Whitfield, Hutchins and my brother Charles were present at our love feast at Fetter Lane with about sixty of our brethren. At about three o'clock in the morning, as we were continuing instant in prayer, the power of God came mightily upon us insomuch that many cried out for exceeding joy, and many fell to the ground. As soon as we were recovered a little from the awe and amazement of His majesty, we broke out with one voice, "We praise Thee, O God! We acknowledge Thee to be the Lord!"[1]

History records that John and Charles Wesley and their prayer partners changed the world by introducing the power of the Holy Spirit through Methodism. Much like the Moravians, the Wesleys were spiritual pioneers who tilled the ground through corporate prayer and planted it with seeds that became a crop of world revival.

The beginning of the twentieth century marked a period of spiritual awakening. History chronicles a revival that began in the hearts of intercessors and swept like wildfire around the world, touching many nations and leaving its mark on the century ahead. In Wales, God laid a burden of prayer on a coal miner named Evan Roberts. One report states that he prayed for thirteen months before the wave of revival came. He prayed until his soul was set on fire; then, he began to declare the message of God. Wherever he preached, heaven resonated in the souls of his listeners. A spirit of conviction fell on the people, and they repented of their sins.

This Welsh Revival had less than a score of intercessors—mainly widows—when it set the population of Wales afire in 1904. The churches were crowded for more than two years, with a hundred thousand souls converted to Christ. Drunkenness was cut in half. Many taverns went bankrupt. Crime diminished, and many policemen were unemployed. The great evangelist Smith Wigglesworth emerged from this revival, which swept across national boundaries, spilling outward and eventually affecting the world.

The Azusa Street Revival, which is credited with ushering in the twentieth-century Pentecostal movement, began with a small band of prayer warriors interceding for revival to come to the city of Los Angeles, California, in 1905. Its impact also was felt around the world. Papa (William J.) Seymour, a pastor seeking all that God was pouring out, went to Charles Fox Parham's Bible school in Houston.

> When Seymour learned that Parham would be remaining in Houston and opening a short-term Bible school, he applied for enrollment. Because of southern segregation laws and customs, his application posed a problem. Parham, nonetheless, skirted the legal restrictions by arranging for Seymour to sit in an adjoining room where, through an open door, he was able to listen to the lectures.[2]

Then he was invited to Los Angeles to begin a work there.

God used Papa Seymour, a wonderful black prophet. He was a humble man who prayed for revival, and he welcomed the Holy Spirit. The revival was multiracial—people of prayer who were black, Hispanic, Asian and white all prayed together. As the revival took off, people from all denominations came and participated. The electricity of the revival began lifting when people broke off into religious sectarianism and racism. All denominations came to drink from it for a while until people started bringing their own religious prescriptions to it.

Now God is raising up new watchmen who will reap the next harvest through prayer. These prayer warriors will be both skilled and equipped to take back their inheritance from the enemy. Today he is calling those who would be watchmen on the wall of prayer.

NEHEMIAH AND THE WALLS OF JERUSALEM

THE BOOK OF Nehemiah contains a picture of what fervent prayer can accomplish in both the spiritual and the natural realms. In a prophetically significant series of actions that took place over a period of fifty-two days, Nehemiah led a band of builders and prayer warriors in the restoration of Jerusalem's walls, which had been ruined at the hands of the Babylonian invaders. Jerusalem's protection against enemies was gone; she lay open to the attack of marauders.

In the natural realm, things looked terrible. The entire city was demolished, the stones of her fortified walls cast down and her gates burned with fire. The people, including Nehemiah, were held captive in Babylonia. Nehemiah served as the king's cupbearer, and he could not leave and begin rebuilding the walls of Jerusalem without first gaining the king's permission.

So Nehemiah fasted and cried out to God in a powerful prayer that began with corporate repentance:

> I beseech thee, O LORD God of heaven, the great and terrible God, that keepeth covenant and mercy for them that love him and observe his commandments: Let thine ear now be attentive, and thine eyes open, that thou mayest hear the prayer of thy servant, which I pray before thee now, day and night, for the children of Israel thy servants, and confess the sins of the children of Israel....Prosper, I pray thee, thy servant this day, and grant him mercy in the sight of this man.
> —NEHEMIAH 1:5–6, 11, KJV

It was not the king's custom to grant such large favors to people in his court. Yet because Nehemiah had prayed and fasted, watching at the wall of prayer night and day, the Lord heard his petitions and granted him extraordinary favor with the king.

Miraculously, permission was granted, and the rebuilding began.

Opposition arises.

But more pitfalls lay ahead. Opposition arose. Sanballat the Horonite and Tobiah the Ammonite, along with others, "all plotted together to come and fight against Jerusalem, to injure and cause confusion and failure in it" (Neh. 4:8, AMP). They stirred up derision, accusation and subversion.

Derision: Sanballat, Tobiah and the others mocked Nehemiah and the builders. Tobiah made fun of their work, saying that if a fox jumped on the wall, it would fall down.

Accusation: They accused Nehemiah of rebellion against the king, and they plotted to kill him.

Subversion: They tried to turn the community against itself, to confuse the builders and turn them against each other. (These types of opposition are important to remember for anyone who starts a watch; do not to be disheartened if these things happen. Just be prepared and keep on holding the watch.)

Focus on God

Nehemiah refused to listen to the enemy or to look at his natural circumstances. He chose to listen to God and look to heaven. Now more fervent prayer was required in order to deal with those who attempted to stop the work that God had called Nehemiah to direct. "Because of them we made our prayer to our God and set a watch against them day and night" (Neh. 4:9, AMP).

Nehemiah positioned men in the breaches in the wall, setting people by families with swords, spears and bows. Then he arose and told everyone, from the nobles to the builders:

> Do not be afraid of the enemy; [earnestly] remember the Lord and imprint Him [on your minds], great and terrible, and [take from Him courage to] fight for your brethren, your sons, your daughters, your wives, and your homes.
> —NEHEMIAH 4:14, AMP

Do not be afraid of whatever the enemy is doing, but focus on the greatness and awesomeness of the Lord Himself. Do not first focus on the enemy; first, focus on the Lord and His greatness.

In the watch, we first exalt the Lord. Whatever else is going on, we look at God first and take courage from Him; then we can look at the enemy and pray over the circumstance. Otherwise our intercessions will be weak-kneed and fearful instead of from a spirit of faith.

One watchman in Michigan had a vision while praying during a watch. He was standing before the banqueting table. The light was extremely intense, and across the table were fields of living green. There were baskets filled with beautiful ripe fruit, a silver pitcher of water and raisin cakes sliced and ready to eat. No matter how much was eaten, the cakes would never get smaller.

An angel spoke to him, "You need to learn to eat from the table." Suddenly, he became aware of what was behind him. The table was set in the presence of his enemies (Ps. 23:5); behind him was blackness. He then understood that it is foolish to be concerned about the circumstances and trials of life. Rather, look in the direction of the banquet table that has been provided for us!

Even in the presence of our enemies, we can look at the Lord and be steeped in His river of anointing, courage and glory. Then we are ready to fight. Then, as we watch, we can fight for our brothers, our sons, our daughters, our wives and our homes... and our church, our neighborhood, our city, our nation.

CONTEMPORARY RUINS

THE RUINS OF the walls of Jerusalem are symbolic of the condition of the society in which we live. One of our Charlotte watchmen shared the following vision, which puts in graphic terms this concept of spiritual ruin:

> I saw a lake of fire with people drowning in it. Their arms were outstretched to anyone who would hear their cry to be pulled out. Around the lake I saw whiskey bottles, syringes used for

illegal drugs, pornographic magazines and birth control devices used in fornication and adultery. The cries coming from the lake were deafening, yet few heard the screams because they were drowned out by television, ball games and other idols of men that cried out for attention. (See Jude 17, 23.)

No one can deny the pain and desolation that exists in America today. Our inner cities are cursed with addiction, poverty, hopelessness and fear. Crime rules many neighborhoods. Our children are dying from violence, drug overdoses, AIDS and various forms of abuse. The enemy has even plundered the homes of many Christians. Divorce is ripping families apart. Sons, daughters and grandchildren are being taken captive—some into perversion, some into drugs, some into cults and the occult. They are denying Christ. Great confusion has swept over our young people.

A Spiritual Vacuum

In the midst of all this brokenness, people are searching for answers. If we, as believers, do not fill the vacuum with the power and glory and presence of God, then the vacuum will be filled with something else—and the spirit of antichrist is just waiting for that opportunity.

At the early part of the century, after the Azusa Street Revival and the Welsh Revival, the major church authorities in Germany actually wrote and signed a document rejecting this move of the Holy Spirit. Essentially, they told the Holy Spirit, "Don't come here." That action created a vacuum in the spirit there. And nature abhors a vacuum—in the physical or the spiritual. Since they rejected the move of the Holy Spirit, there was plenty of room for the spirit of antichrist to move in.

People often wonder, *How could some of the finest people in the world in Germany have allowed the Holocaust to happen?* Well, the spirit of antichrist was able to fully work. The power of the Holy Spirit was turned away.

The same principle applies with our children, in our homes, in the church and in our nation. If we don't fill our lives with God, then the enemy is only too happy to oblige and fill them with destruction. If the watchmen will not stay awake, the city will be taken.

The powers of darkness are determined to steal our inheritance. There is a call to arms against the forces of evil, and the only ones who can effectively wage that war in power are those who know the name of Jesus and are filled with the Holy Spirit. Our mission is to bring down the power and glory of God and to usher in His presence.

"For behold, the darkness shall cover the earth, and deep darkness the people" (Isa. 60:2). Indeed, it is dark on the earth in these days. But there is hope in the body of Christ: "Arise, shine; for your light has come! And the glory of the LORD is risen upon you" (Isa. 60:1). So we need to watch, be alert, be the light. From every church, the light needs to be shining.

ALL BELIEVERS CALLED TO PRAY

JUST AS JESUS wept when He saw the condition of Israel, with her spiritual blindness and desolation, and yearned to gather His children under His protective wing, the Lord today is imparting that same burden to those who will intercede.

In Joel, the call to intercession goes out to everyone—from the priests who minister at the altar to the mothers at home nursing infants. In Nehemiah, all the families came to repair the wall. The need is too great and the battle too intense for just a few to be expected to carry the burden. When we truly see the great extent of the need on earth today, and how much every nation is affected by prayer—or its absence—we will see how important our own individual prayers of intercession are in the process of God's work on earth. This church is called to watch and pray, as the Lord showed a watchman here in Charlotte through this vision:

I saw walls made of bricks representing the church. As we worshiped and praised in spiritual warfare, the walls came down,

brick by brick. They were thrown into a fiery kiln. The fire puri-
fied and refined the bricks, removing those things that had
gotten mixed in with the truth. Out of the fire came golden
bricks. These bricks were used to build the walls of intercession—walls of protection against the enemy, walls around cities
of refuge, designed to keep the enemy out, but welcoming in all
who would seek shelter.

In the history of Israel, when the priests went before the Lord,
they stood on behalf of the entire nation. They did not come to the
altar of God to get their own needs met. They stood in the gap for
the needs of all the people; they carried the nation of Israel in their
hearts. This is the essence of all intercession—coming before God on
behalf of others. Healing for our nations will be released as God's
chosen people stand before Him in prayer under the prophetic
cloud of His presence.

In the New Testament, God clearly places this mantle of prayer
upon the shoulders of all believers. John testified that Jesus "has
made us kings and priests to His God and Father, to Him be glory
and dominion forever and ever" (Rev. 1:6). Peter referred to believers
as "a spiritual house, an holy priesthood, to offer up spiritual sacrifices, acceptable to God through Jesus Christ...a chosen generation,
a royal priesthood, an holy nation" (1 Pet. 2:5, 9, KJV).

The aspects of the former priestly ministry were shadows of the
anointing of the Holy Spirit. This anointing is the promise that was
to come to the heirs of salvation in Christ. In the new blood
covenant in Christ we have received a living mantle of priesthood.
As we pray before the Lord, we have this authority, not because we
know all the principles, not because we have done everything right,
not because we haven't fallen or failed, but because Jesus has
washed us in His blood and made us His priests to minister His
anointing.

In Joel the Lord has given us a model of intercession:

Drunks, wake up and cry! All you people who drink wine,

cry! . . . Cry as a young woman cries when the man she is going to marry has died. . . . Cry loudly, you who grow grapes. Cry for the wheat and the barley. Cry because the harvest of the field is lost.
—JOEL 1:5, 8, 11, NCV

In other words, pray for others as if we were praying for our own most heartfelt needs.

Thus, during the Watch of the Lord, we lay aside our own burdens and concerns in order to pray for the needs of our cities, our nation and our world. This is not a "bless me" club; it's a battle in the spiritual realm against the powers of darkness at work in our land. It's hand-to-hand combat against the powers of the Antichrist.

A WATCHMAN FOR EVERY HOUSE

LOOK TO THE Lord great and terrible, and take from Him the courage to fight. Look to the Lord, you who have been abused, you who have been oppressed. Look to the Lord and imprint Him onto your hearts and minds. You are sons and daughters of the King—the Lion of the tribe of Judah. Take from Him your courage to fight for your sons and daughters, husbands and wives, homes and families.

Every household should have a watchman—every church, every city, every family. With the coming of the Lord at hand, this call is urgent. It's a wake-up call. As you watch, the glory of the Lord will shine upon you. But if you slumber in this hour, the city will be taken.

Fight for your sons and daughters. This is an emergency call to our nation. The devil is trying to take our children captive with drugs, dark music, loneliness and depression. The demons attacking families are murder, death, hate, anger, racism and more. If we as parents and the Spirit-filled church don't pray, our children will be taken.

As watchmen we must get on the walls on behalf of our children. If you don't have children, pray for your neighbor's children and the kids in your youth group. Every child needs to be covered. The watch is one of the primary ways we can do this.

Who will answer the call to fight and protect our kids through prayer? The whole reason for prayer is persons! The Lord says, in the last verses of the Old Testament:

> Behold, I will send you Elijah the prophet before the coming of the great and dreadful day of the LORD. And he will turn the hearts of the fathers to the children, and the hearts of the children to their fathers, lest I come and strike the earth with a curse.
> —MALACHI 4:5–6

The Spirit of the Lord wants to keep a curse from coming upon our children. They are exposed, ready to be taken by the enemy. Prayer is the first step toward protection. The families must gather at the breach.

A WATCHMAN FOR EVERY SCHOOL

WE MUST COVER the schools in prayer. Spiritually, we can enforce the authority of the Lord Jesus over the schools. Where your children attend school is your God-given sphere of responsibility, and you have authority to pray over it. Exercise that authority regularly, covering your children with a hedge of prayer (Hos. 2:5–7).

Psychologists, mental health workers and school administrators can do what they know how to do. But unless we lift up the children, the strongholds of darkness will not be demolished. Who is praying for the kids in trouble? Lift them up; bind the powers of darkness. The strongholds from the dark music, the death culture, witchcraft and the occult—these are the spiritual forces attacking our children. Only the power of the Holy Spirit and the mighty name of Jesus, will pull down the strongholds.

> For though we walk (live) in the flesh, we are not carrying on our warfare according to the flesh and using mere human weapons. For the weapons of our warfare are not physical [weapons of flesh and blood], but they are mighty before God for the overthrow and destruction of strongholds.
> —2 CORINTHIANS 10:3–4, AMP

"They may have taken prayer out of schools, but they cannot take schools out of prayer!" I heard the Lord say this as we started interceding for our local schools during our watch. The legislatures have taken God out of schools. Now that breach has become the responsibility and the opportunity of the believing church. The watch can rebuild the broken places in society that are leaving our children exposed to destruction by the enemy.

I'm calling for there to be a watch for every school, especially in public schools. If your child or grandchild is in school, you are God's watchman-intercessor for that school. You don't need to be "led" to pray for that school; it is your *duty* to pray for the school. Take an active, alert role walking back and forth on the wall, vigilant in the anointing. Prayer has become a passive thing, but to be a watchman is to be active and alert.

Watch alone, if necessary, but preferably in groups of two or more. Mom and Dad, gather with other interested believing parents and grandparents. Pray for physical safety and protection for your children so that the children may learn in safety. Bind the satanic spirits of violence, occult, drugs, perversion, rebellion, racism, hate and the music and culture of death and suicide. Release the peace and anointing of the precious Holy Spirit of God. Release the holy angels of God to stand guard over that school day and night.

> For we are not wrestling with flesh and blood...but against the despotisms, against the powers, against [the master spirits who are] the world rulers of this present darkness, against the spirit forces of wickedness in the heavenly (supernatural) sphere.
> —EPHESIANS 6:12, AMP

Include your child's school in your daily individual prayers and weekly corporate prayers at your watch and at church. Perhaps a number of believing parents could gather in a room at the school to pray for the school. Where this is not possible, pray outside the school; walk around it or drive around it, claiming the school for God. Release angels to watch and protect each child.

Find out names of troubled students from your children, those who are troublemakers or threatening violence. Make a prayer list and pray for them by name. Pray also for the lonely, abused or depressed teens.

This generation of teens is so tender toward the Lord—the most tender I have seen. We pray for all the youth in our church by name every week. This is an important generation! Watch and pray for them.

A WATCHMAN FOR EVERY CITY

I BELIEVE GOD had some special purposes in mind when He revealed to us that we were to hold the Watch of the Lord each Friday night. Much of the crime and violence that takes place in our cities happens on the weekends. When we gather to pray on Friday night, we spread out a map of our city and pray over the map. We pray for Charlotte. We pray for her people. Some of our watchmen actually gather around the map, spread out on the floor, and lay on top of it, praying in deep intercession and travail.

We pray, "Lord, we are the 'Secret Service' over this city—Your 'Secret Service.' Show us how to pray. Show the Charlotte police where the drug dealers are. Show the police where crimes are about to be committed. Lead them right there!"

We are reclaiming the weekends for Christ. We pray often for our city. In the March 4, 1999, *Charlotte Observer* was an article titled "Counties' Crime Rate Continues Steady Drop." The article stated that residents are safer now than any year since 1980. Bonnie and I believe that our prayers for our city had something to do with those lowered crime statistics.

As we pray for our cities, the Lord will move, and one by one our cities will be reclaimed for Christ and His purposes. He will bring redemption and restoration to those areas that were ravaged by the enemy. Here is what one of our watchmen saw as we prayed together:

> The Lord showed me many cities. I recognized London because of Big Ben and New York City because of the Empire

State Building. I saw these cities shrouded in a black veil, and the buildings looked gray and dirty. Then the veil started to peel and split down the middle. Above it was a glorious light that was pushing and tearing the veil. Then the buildings looked clean and new as the light shone on them.

This is the kind of power we can expect to exert on a city, a nation and the world as we stand in the gap and begin to bind the strongmen in control of our cities and streets.

WATCHMEN, GO FORTH!

FOR A LONG time the church held times of fellowship where we ate cake together, said a little prayer, sang a few songs and went home. Those times are over. The church at the end of the age will be manifested as the bride of Christ, fit to reign beside the King of kings. The Lord wants to give us the nations for an inheritance; to Bonnie and me, that means He wants to enable us to effectively preach the gospel to the nations with signs and wonders. But first, we must yield to His call to watch and pray.

God will show us how to pray. In His grace He allows us to participate and help fulfill His strategies for the nations, just as He did this watchman in Georgia:

> The Lord gave me a vision of a jail cell with the people of North Korea standing inside the cell. Satan was standing guard outside the jail door. The church was also standing on the outside of the jail cell with the key to the door. We were ready to unlock the door; however, Satan was upset and growling at the church.

We must pray Satan away from the nations to allow the light of the gospel in. But like the ten virgins in Jesus' parable, only the wise will buy this costly oil of prayer and be ready, lamps burning, when Jesus appears. We have a responsibility as believers not only to get ourselves ready, but to call out to others to do the same.

Anyone with a heart for the nations is called to help. In fact, keeping the Watch of the Lord is one way such individuals can "go" into the world and minister to the lost in faraway places. As you consistently watch and pray for those who are sent and the nations where they are sent, you are like the early Moravians—like the one at home praying for the one on the field. Be faithful as watchmen at home, that God will enable you to put your feet in the field.

All it takes is to share our vision for the Watch of the Lord and to make the commitment to watch and pray.

❦

Bless the LORD,
all you servants of the LORD,
who by night stand in the
house of the LORD!

———

—PSALM 134:1

Corporate Prayer and Intercession

♣

THIS VISION WAS given to one of our watchmen in Montgomery, Alabama:

Corporate Prayer releasing strong Prophetic anointing

I was standing at the edge of an enormous dirt field that stretched in all directions as far as the eye could see. Somehow I knew I was supposed to go and work that field, that the owner wanted the whole acreage cultivated, planted and prepared for harvest. I looked across that great expanse of earth to see if it was really as vast as my first impression, and indeed it was.

In the distance I could see a few other workers. Separated by wide distances, these workers were tending their respective patches of land with great diligence. Even though I thought I didn't have much of a chance of succeeding, out of responsibility to my Boss, I put my hand to the task of working a little spot of land. Maybe He would send more workers.

I looked down and noticed that I was holding a small shovel.

Something was written on it in tiny letters. I had to hold it close to my face in order to read what it said. Squinting, I made out the word *prayer*. That inscription told me three things—that prayer was definitely the tool to use in this field; that something was lacking in the quantity and quality of my prayer life; and that everyone else in the field had the same tool as mine. Thinking that someday I might get a bigger shovel, I bent down and went to work.

Just like in the movies, time lapsed, and suddenly I was looking down at two tomato plants. One actually had a little green tomato clinging to its vine. The second plant seemed to have some potential, and I was already beginning to work a third plant. *Aha!* I thought. *Two and a half feet high! Progress!* I was proud of my little plants, and I returned to my labors with my tiny prayer-shovel in hand.

Suddenly I heard the deafening growl of a gigantic engine. I popped my head up, and there it was—reverberating with power, smoke billowing from its huge exhaust pipes—the most enormous tractor/combine I had ever seen. Not only was it impressive, it was also scary. I stared at the machine, right there at the edge of the field, and listened to its engines roar. By my quick calculations, I realized that what the others and I could not finish in a lifetime, this thing could accomplish in a matter of days.

Just then a jolly-looking gentleman poked his head out of the driver's compartment and called out to me, "Working the field?"

"Yes sir, I am."

"Need any help?"

"Yes sir," I answered. "I actually do. Can this rig of yours plow?"

"Yep."

"Plant?"

"Yep."

"Fertilize?"

74

"Yep."

"Water, too?"

"Yes, it's real good at that."

But I figured it probably could not do one thing, so I asked, "Can it weed?"

"Yep; it does it all. Better get on board."

So I did, even though I hated to leave my puny little plants. I climbed up into the cab and joined the nice man there. "Hey," I asked, "who are you?"

His eyes twinkling, he grinned and said, "The Boss sent me."

"Well," I said, "What is this thing you're driving?"

"Oh, this?" He patted the dashboard affectionately and replied, "This baby is corporate prayer!"

God is harvesting the globe for souls and using corporate prayer as a great tool to ease the way and make short work of this otherwise mammoth undertaking.

A New Word for Today

THE LORD IS releasing a new word on an old subject. The old subject is prayer, and the new word is, "Pray corporately!" The Lord is opening our eyes to a simple truth: Prayer is where everything begins and ends in the realm of the Spirit. It's where everything is accomplished.

Prayer—communion with God—is the true genetic code of the church, her very backbone. A falling away from prayer, which happened over many generations, is what caused the church to fall away gradually from God's true design for His body. Only prayer will bring us back.

As we pressed into God in prayer in 1995, we began to pick up His heartbeat. He revealed to us that corporate prayer is the most important type of prayer there is, that those who consistently spend time praying together will notice certain changes taking place. Their perspective, endurance, patience and many other factors will be affected for good. Genuine love, appreciation for and cooperation with each other will increase. And this is not to mention the answers one will get from prayer.

Consistent corporate prayer has also been known to break down supernaturally the denominational walls of partition among the body of Christ. For instance, the watch in Cairo, Egypt, is composed of Protestants, Catholics and people from the Orthodox church. In America as well, different denominations, including some that are very traditional, are getting together to watch.

A LESSER PART OF A GREATER WHOLE

GOD WANTS US to unite in prayer. Satan's strategy is to divide and conquer. A divided family, city or nation will fall. But God's house shall stand; it is His house of prayer. Once we as a body learn to take this to heart and pray together, in unison, we will see a great outpouring of revival that will become stronger and stronger until it virtually covers the globe.

The Lord has shown us clearly that people, particularly in the church in the West, need to move their personal agendas out of the way; thus, they will merge into God's bigger plan. This is critical on the heart of God. One of the worst mistakes we can make is to hold onto the spirit of independence, because it will cut us off from the virtue of God. It deceives us into thinking that we are islands; it forces us to concentrate on our failures and weaknesses. Then we become even more isolated and alienated—a downward cycle of losing.

For those of us from the charismatic era, this is a good word. We are grateful for all the positive things the charismatic movement brought to the church, when the things of the Spirit became a fresh experience for so many Christians. But some of its weaknesses are now being remedied.

Things went inward to a great degree; they were focused on "me," as if God's whole purpose were to make *me* feel better, to give *me* spiritual gifts. One evidence of that is that thousands of new churches were birthed, but just a tiny amount of their resources were tracked as going into any kind of missions work—into reaching the unreached, which is actually the commission of the church!

The charismatic era as we knew it produced Lone Rangers. It bred the spirit of independence and put God's stamp of approval on it. "Look at me; I speak in tongues, I pray for the sick and they get well."

Now the Lord is lassoing all the Lone Rangers, taking off their masks and shooting their horses. One of the new things that God is doing is building a family, a corporate body of believers.

We want to hold this revelation that we are members of one another and be strengthened daily by that. In so doing, we are touching and agreeing with others in prayer, losing our individual identities in favor of a corporate one. We effectively exchange our independence for interdependence. As this exchange takes place on earth in prayer, powerful things happen in the realm of the spirit.

During a watch in Charlotte, one watchman saw gears, both large and small, rotating in a watch. The gears represent us—some larger and stronger, some smaller and weaker. But when we all move together in the Lord's timing, we usher in the next move of the Holy Spirit. We must work together in harmony, doing our parts.

The corporate watch is the dynamic that has caused so much revelation of the real Jesus to come into individual people's lives—and has changed them! We need to attach ourselves to other intercessors, to go to where the watchmen are gathering together and become a part of that whole, interceding as one body in the Lord. In order to do that, we must understand what intercession is—and what it isn't.

INTERCESSION—MYTHS AND TRUTHS

As I HAVE said, Bonnie and I see intercession as one aspect of prayer. For a long time now intercession has been shrouded in mystery. Treated as a special calling that only a few could attain, intercession has not been a popular subject within the church. Christians are quick to say, "That isn't my calling!" After all, who wants to spend time groaning and fasting and weeping and praying? Is that what you think intercession is?

As we watch and pray, there are occasions when the Lord will corporately lay on our hearts the need to come to the altar for a season of tears, travail and repentance. As you remember, in Joel the priests were invited to "weep between the porch and the altar" in the time of desolation so that God would pour out the rain of the Holy Spirit to bring restoration (2:17). We have seasons in which the Holy Spirit gives us the burden to "pray through" for our children, our church, our city and our nation. This is a supernatural burden, and after a season of groanings and tears, it lifts, and we are led into praise and thanksgiving.

In the last several years as we have watched faithfully for hours each week, we have learned some valuable lessons on true intercession. Prayer watch leaders and pastors need to keep a sharp, alert eye and ear when they participate in seasons of repentance or travail. Some people may come to the prayer meeting with their own agendas, heartbreaks and distresses. But there will be a clear difference between people releasing their own discouragements and fears and Spirit-led tears. While there may be a need for that release in the individual's life, the prayer watch is not the place.

A prayer watch captain must be alert to this difference. Spirit-led tears are powerful in intercession; however, soulish emotionalism and travail will attempt to kill a prayer watch. If a wet blanket of unbelief and sadness descends over your prayer watch, a brief exhortation of the greatness and faithfulness of our Lord and Savior, Jesus Christ, and a few praise songs will get you back into the atmosphere of faith, which is the oxygen of the Watch of the Lord.

Some people even think of intercession as this emotional, discouraging travail, but that's a misconception. Others have a concept of intercession that has been formed primarily by their image of an angry, Old Testament God on the brink of pouring out punishment for sin. If this image is accurate, then Christ, who according to Isaiah 53 was punished for our sins, died in vain. This religious concept of God colors much of the church's experience. But today we serve the true God under the New Covenant through the blood of Jesus in the fullness of the Holy Spirit.

> But you have not come to the mountain [Sinai] that may be touched and that burned with fire, and to blackness and darkness and tempest, and the sound of a trumpet and the voice of words, so that those who heard it begged that the word should not be spoken to them anymore.... But you have come to Mount Zion and to the city of the living God, the heavenly Jerusalem, to an innumerable company of angels, to the general assembly and church of the firstborn who are registered in heaven, to God the Judge of all, to the spirits of just men made perfect, to Jesus the Mediator of the new covenant, and to the blood of sprinkling that speaks better than that of Abel.
>
> —HEBREWS 12:18–19, 22–24

It's important to remember that as we approach the end of the age we are in the season of the bride being prepared for her Husband. "For lo, the winter is past" (Song of Sol. 2:11). Spring is coming—a season of joy and singing and restoration, full of promise. So intercession begins with exalting the Lord, and that is celebratory. We exalt the Lord first, then the darkness doesn't seem so dark. The Holy Spirit is the Comforter. In His presence is fullness of joy. If there is a time of travail, it is specifically led by the Holy Spirit.

The difference between that dark, old intercessory tone and the current bright tone is perfectly illustrated in the situation in John 8 in which the righteous religious men brought a woman caught in adultery to Jesus. The Law said to stone her, and everyone knew it. Besides that, God was the One who wrote the Law.

But standing before the guilty woman was her penalty for that sin: Jesus Himself. Therefore He could extend to her forgiveness. His solution was not stoning, though that was a just punishment. No, Jesus' solution for her sin was to tell her, "Neither do I condemn you; go and sin no more" (v. 11). In saying He did not condemn her, Jesus was telling her that He did not judge against her or sentence her. As the Lamb slain before the foundation of the world, Jesus had become her sentence, her condemnation for sin as the ultimate Intercessor.

Jesus, the living God, became living Word, and that living Word was completely different from what the people governed by the Law would have given. We're finding the same thing happening in the real presence of the Lord today. The nature and spirit of our message under this New Covenant is as different from that of the Old as day is from night. God has not changed, but He did change the conditions of His relationship to man. Instead of the Law, He instituted the eternal contract of reconciliation with us through His Son. Our New Covenant has a different spirit from the Old Covenant—a spirit of life rather than death.

Suddenly the living Lord of the church is stepping into church business. We must hear what He is saying, and it may not be what we expected. The living presence has not been in our midst before as it is now. We do what the living Christ tells us, whether it is the way we did it before or not. He is drawing us into His living love. His voice is redemptive. He is wooing us with His glory.

THE SEASON OF THE BRIDE

ANYONE CAN TELL you that no woman would be wooed by a man who constantly criticizes, rebukes, rejects, corrects or abuses her. A bride is wooed by love. Love is the message of the New Covenant. This is the season of God's outpoured love wooing this woman—the church, His bride to be. The true bride will receive His love and, in return, will extend her hands of mercy and redemption in the same spirit to those who need forgiveness, rather than judgment. Jesus is moving heaven and earth to woo back His unfaithful wife.

We believe there's a changing of the guard; the Lord is leaving the old traditions behind. The season for harshness and judgment of sin is not now, though a lot of voices cry out to the contrary. Too many other signs are attesting to the nature of God as revealed in Hosea 2, the mercy of the Lord, where He's causing the heavens and the earth to allure humanity and bring us to Himself:

> "Therefore, behold, I will allure her, will bring her into the wilderness, and speak comfort to her. I will give her her vineyards from there, and the Valley of Achor as a door of hope; she shall sing there, as in the days of her youth, as in the day when she came up from the land of Egypt.
> "And it shall be, in that day," says the LORD, "that you will call Me 'My Husband,' and no longer call Me 'My Master.'"
> —HOSEA 2:14–16

The goodness of God leads to repentance. That's an ongoing, living theme in almost every watch.

INTERCESSION IS BEING, NOT DOING

INTERCESSION IS NOT so much something we *do;* instead, it is a place of *being*. It takes discipline, yes, and commitment, but it is joyous and full of experiences of God's glory. As we seek God, intercession comes naturally.

When we intercede, we put ourselves in the breach in the wall.

> So I sought for a man among them who would make a wall, and stand in the gap before Me on behalf of the land, that I should not destroy it.
> —EZEKIEL 22:30

An intercessor is someone who stands in the breach, not someone with a long list. We need to interrupt that idea. The intercessor stands as a mediary in the broken-down place, between God's purposes and what is actually happening on earth, between God and those who justly deserve God's judgment. Standing in the breach is automatically doing the work of intercession.

When we are positioned in the gap for our families, our churches, our cities and our nation, then the *words* of intercession will come. Intercession is not about saying the right words; it's about being in the right place at the right time with God. The work of prayer proceeds out of that, but it will then be a work of the Spirit, not the flesh. God provides for us the spirit of intercession in which we can flow, like a river.

> Unless the LORD builds the house, they labor in vain who build it; unless the LORD guards the city, the watchman stays awake in vain.
>
> —PSALM 127:1

This psalm shows us that the action of the watchman is simply to be present at his post, vigilant and faithful. But the progress of the building and the protection for the city come from the presence, power and intervention of the Lord, and not from the strength of man. This is why the atmosphere of the watch can be anticipated as a "date" with Jesus. He has already accomplished the labor to save through His death, burial and resurrection, so it's no longer labor for us.

JESUS AS INTERCESSOR

JESUS WAS THE ultimate Intercessor on the cross. Intercession didn't have to do with anything He *said*. He just *was* the Intercessor.

On the cross Jesus didn't spout off a laundry list of people's sins and diseases so that God would take His eraser and erase them all. No, His body *was* the sacrifice. He *was* the Intercessor. His body was put in the breach for every sin, for every bit of brokenness and every tear, and He became those things as He hung in the breach for us. He is the ultimate pattern of the intercessor, and at the cross, He brought redemption.

Jesus at the cross poured out His soul, His blood; He was numbered with the transgressors. He bore our sins; He made intercession for those who were crucifying Him: "Father, forgive them." So the judgment that was due them came upon Him (Isa. 53:12).

Intercession is the primary aspect of Jesus' life right now: "Therefore He is also able to save to the uttermost those who come to God through Him, since He always lives to make intercession for them" (Heb. 7:25). "One man of you shall chase a thousand, for the LORD your God is He who fights for you, as He has promised you" (Josh. 23:10). For thirty years He lived a family life; then He had three and a half years of public ministry. For the two thousand years since then, His ministry has been intercession!

> [The Lord] saw that there was no man,
> And wondered that there was no intercessor;
> Therefore His own arm brought salvation for Him;
> And His own righteousness, it sustained Him.
>
> —ISAIAH 59:16

This scripture points out that God Himself became the Intercessor. It also shows that the major responsibility believers have toward both God and man is to be intercessors. As we get into that relational place of being the intercessor, the work of prayer flows naturally as the by-product of being an intercessor.

INTIMACY LEADS TO INTERCESSION

ABRAHAM HIMSELF WAS an intercessor for Lot and his family, pleading for them regarding the imminent destruction of Sodom. Moses had Aaron stand as high priest between God and the destruction of Israel. He stood in the gap on behalf of the very people who had accused them; he stood between the living and the dead, and the plague was stopped (Num. 16:41–48).

All these intercessors, from Abraham to Moses to Jesus, were on very intimate terms with God. It was because of their intimacy that they could stand between the living and the dead, that they could be intercessors. So we emphasize intimacy in the watch, intimacy that gives us the place to be intercessors. No intimacy, no intercession. Intimacy is a major key; it gives us the ability to stand in the presence of the Lord with reverence and intercede for people.

These persons in the Bible who stood as intercessors basically said, "Lord, don't be angry; don't punish these people." By nature, an intercessor is one who, because he knows God intimately, understands that the true heart of God is *not* to mete out punishment in anger.

Intercessors were the ones who knew the Lord well enough to know that if they asked Him, He would relent from allowing evil to come onto people. They had a revelation of who God really was, not a first impression as someone who knew God casually would have. He was their Friend, Father, Savior. When you are intimate with the heart of God, you know that He loves people—you know His total compassion, His heart to save mankind.

We can get a Jonah spirit, which is not congruent with the Lord. Even though Jonah was a servant, he took on a judgmental attitude. God's heart was to save the Ninevites, but Jonah didn't want that because the Ninevites were the enemies of the Jews.

God looked with compassion on the Ninevites, who were suffering misery and anguish because of the yoke of sin. So God sent Jonah to Nineveh—not because He was angry, but because of the people's misery—to tell them to stop sinning.

The people heard God and turned from their evil ways. Then God relented from the disaster that He said would come upon them. Jonah was reluctant to be a "wall of prayer" for Nineveh, because he knew that God would relent and extend forgiveness, mercy and love, even for a people who were Jonah's public enemy number one. Jonah made a poor choice, but in his choice we can see what he knew about the compassionate heart of God: His desire was to relent.

All these men knew that in His heart, God didn't really want to destroy these people. Like any father, I can get quite angry with my children, but I totally love them. God gets angry with us, too. And as with human fathers, if someone with "reason" can intervene, the wrath can be stemmed.

ATOMIC PRAYER POWER

OUR TASK IS simply to come together and harmonize in the presence of the Lord, making ourselves available to love on Him, standing in the gap as intercessors, waiting until He shows up and obeying His instructions. Then every prayer will be led by the Holy Spirit. Bonnie and I have learned throughout the years of our ministry every prayer led by the Holy Spirit will touch the heart of God!

If much can be done in the realm of the spirit when just two people agree on earth, as Matthew 18:19 states, consider all that can be done when more than two gather for the purpose of prayer. God wants to release the atomic power of prayer, like a bomb. And He can do that when a hundred people fast food and sleep and stay up all night, caught up before Him in fervent prayer. There is something about agreement in prayer that intensifies its power.

Bonnie and I call that atomic release of the power of God "reaching critical mass." Prayer, like water from a storm or atomic particles around the core of a reactor, gathers into one great mass. We must keep collecting it until, at precisely the right time, it goes *boom!* When prayer reaches critical mass, an atomic explosion occurs in the heavenly realm and things change here on earth. It's not ours to determine when it reaches critical mass; we must keep collecting it. At the right time, it will explode. BOOM!

the sound of prayer

DWELLING TOGETHER IN UNITY

INCREDIBLE THINGS HAPPEN when people pray corporately. In corporate prayer there is protection, increase and an easy yoke. In the environment of corporate prayer, those who pray together surrender their independence and become a picture of "the two as one"— agreement among believers. Only as the bride of Christ is prepared and released into the knowledge that there is neither Jew nor Greek, bond nor free, male nor female in God's kingdom will the real power come.

In 1998 a watchmen in Democratic Republic of Congo in Africa received this vision during worship:

> A great multitude of people were entering a city. They were from every race, and each one was dressed in his own way. Some were barefoot, without shirts or shorts; others had shoes and shirts, without trousers. They had arrows, axes and hoes. Everyone had his own language. They were a crowd of invaders without a leader.
>
> The Holy Spirit said, "This is how the church looks today. Pray that the church will be united, with the same mind and thought, and that they will walk in the same direction under the lordship of Jesus and the leadership of the Holy Spirit; then shall My power be manifested."

Where brethren dwell together in unity, God commands the blessing (Ps. 133:1). It thrills God's heart for people in one accord to get together. Corporate prayer is not for people who are fighting in groups and sects. It is for those who can be of one heart. In Acts 2, when the disciples gathered together in one accord, the Holy Spirit came. That's atomic prayer power. The power of the Holy Spirit is released when people are together in one accord.

Practically speaking, it is so much easier for one hundred men to build a house than for one man to attempt the job. The work—the practical burden and responsibility—is easier when it's spread across everyone; it's easier for the individual, faster for the project and much more efficient and effective. The combining of multiple talents, multiple people receiving revelation and multiple people exercising their faith make each individual's part of the burden much lighter.

Because of the fellowship, you cease fighting the battle alone. The encouragement and strength of others empower you. Plus, you learn how to be part of the whole and work with others. That gives you the benefits of a corporate vision rather that leaning on just your own perspective of the revelation.

> For as the body is one and has many members, but all the members of that one body, being many, are one body, so also is Christ.
>
> —1 CORINTHIANS 12:12

If we can form groups of people from town to town, city to city and nation to nation around the world who can carry the anointing and pray powerfully as a corporate body, we can change things and truly become God's ambassadors on the earth.

THE COMMITMENT OF CORPORATE PRAYER

GETTING IN TOUCH with the heart of God, however, is going to involve sacrifice. It means putting down our own agendas and ambitions and picking up the heartbeat of His kingdom. In this hour, God is saying, "Forget about your ministry and your gifts; forget about finances; forget about wanting to get married. It is time to seek the Lord."

In the Charismatic movement, we followed the spiritual fad of the week just as we listened to the tape of the week. We went from one fad to another, and that's OK for children. But when people grow up, they don't flip from one thing to another. Watching is fun and exciting, but it's also long-term. We're going to watch and pray till Jesus comes. The bride will be a watching, praying bride when Jesus arrives to take her away.

There is inevitably a certain amount of work associated with prayer. Call it "groundwork," if you like. A builder does not begin to set in the framework for the walls until a foundation has first been laid. The work of prayer begins with a commitment that must be kept, regardless of how we feel.

Prayer also takes time. It involves setting priorities and then keeping them as a continual focus. That's why, once we commit to becoming a watchman on the wall, we need so much grace. Distractions will be deliberately sent from the enemy's camp, designed to pull us away from our commitment and cause us to focus on seemingly more important matters. We must not leave the task before it's finished. And it won't be finished until the gospel has been proclaimed with signs following in every nation. Then Jesus will appear. Jesus said concerning watching and praying, "When the Son of Man comes, will He really find faith on the earth?" (Luke 18:8).

Heed His call to watch on the wall of prayer and rebuild what was left to ruin during previous prayerless generations. Those who get the vision for changing the world will be those who find the yoke of watching and praying an easy one to bear. It's a privilege. In fact, it's a calling.

§

Naomi . . . said to her,
"My daughter, shall I not seek
security for you, that it may be well with you? . . .
Therefore wash yourself and anoint yourself,
put on your best garment and go
down to the threshing floor."

———————

—RUTH 3:1, 3

6

The Bride in the Watch

---

§

I T WAS DURING our first Watch of the Lord in Charlotte in 1995 that I saw a vision of feet—big feet. "Lord, do You want me to pray for feet? The healing of feet? Does someone here tonight have athlete's foot? What does this mean?"

I got nothing. Big feet. That's all.

The following week I again had the same vision—only this time I saw clouds around the feet. Feet and clouds and nothing else. The meaning was still a mystery.

During our third Friday night watch the vision came again. This time I could see that the clouds were alive—gold and white and full of rolling movement and lightnings. They were full of blessing, with such love in them. The clouds weren't threatening, just full of love. Suddenly the clouds dispersed; for only a moment, I could see nail prints in those big feet. Then the word of the Lord came to me, saying, "Go to Ruth, chapter 3." In my spirit, I also heard the Lord in the Person of the Holy Spirit say, "My voice is the voice of Naomi."

I immediately turned to the Book of Ruth, pondering what God had just said. Then, as I read from chapter 3, I saw the picture:

> Then Naomi her mother-in-law said to her, "My daughter, shall I not seek security for you, that it may be well with you? Now Boaz, whose young women you were with, is he not our relative? In fact, he is winnowing barley tonight at the threshing floor. Therefore wash yourself and anoint yourself, put on your best garment and go down to the threshing floor; but do not make yourself known to the man until he has finished eating and drinking. Then it shall be, when he lies down, that you shall notice the place where he lies; and you shall go in, uncover his feet, and lie down; and he will tell you what you should do."
>
> —RUTH 3:1–4

Naomi, Ruth's mother-in-law, was seeking Ruth's welfare, just as the Holy Spirit seeks our well-being. This concept—Naomi as a type of the Holy Spirit—was entirely new to me. I had never heard any teaching to that effect. Naomi wanted Ruth to have security as a wife and mother, and she realized that Boaz, the kinsman-redeemer, was the one who would provide it.

A NIGHT AT THE FEET OF BOAZ

RUTH WAS OBEDIENT. She bathed, put on perfume, dressed in her best garment and went to the threshing floor as instructed. There she waited. For a few short hours the evening breeze hastened the winnowing process by blowing the chaff away. The men laughed and talked as they worked. There was food and wine. Harvest was always a time of celebration.

Ruth watched the men as they ate and drank, and she listened to their laughter. When the breeze died down and the merriment stopped, Boaz lay down next to his pile of grain and fell asleep. Ruth went to where he was lying, uncovered his feet and lay down quietly.

92

At midnight Boaz turned in his sleep, awoke and discovered her at his feet.

"Take your maidservant under your wing," she said, which was her simple yet unmistakable proposal of marriage. She was telling him, "I want to be yours. I want to be under your protection, under your covering."

Boaz responded with a promise, "Do not fear. I will do for you all that you request... Stay this night..." (vv. 9–13). His words told Ruth that she had stolen his heart by her actions. He was thrilled that she chose him over the younger men, and he promised to marry her. Then Boaz told her what to do next.

As I pondered these passages in relation to the vision of the feet and clouds, I realized that Naomi, as a type of the Holy Spirit, was telling us that it is now time to prepare ourselves to spend the night at the feet of our Kinsman-Redeemer, Jesus Christ. Just like Boaz, Jesus rejoices when we choose Him over the distractions and enticements of the world. At His feet, we will receive instruction regarding His every desire for us. At His threshing floor, He winnows us, removing chaff from our lives, and grooms us into His bride.

When Ruth left in the morning, Boaz heaped grain in her shawl for her to carry home to Naomi. We have discovered that in the same way, our heavenly Boaz heaps His blessing on us as we spend the night at His feet.

A DATE WITH JESUS

FROM THE VISIONS of the feet and the revelation from the Book of Ruth, it became clear to me that we needed to prepare ourselves, just as Ruth did, to meet the Lover of our souls—to have a date with Jesus. He has entered into not only a covenant relationship with us, His church, but also a love relationship. Teenagers have dates on Friday nights. Why shouldn't we meet with our Bridegroom then, too?

We must prepare for our date as Ruth did, as all those anticipating time with their Beloved do.

93

Wash ourselves.

We cleanse ourselves through the Word of God, allowing it to purify our hearts and reveal any sin that needs to be washed away. The bride of Christ is to be without spot or wrinkle (Eph. 5:27). A lifestyle of repentance is part of humbling ourselves in the presence of the Lord.

Anoint ourselves.

We have available to us the sweet perfumed oil of the outpouring of the Holy Spirit. We are to come into the flow of the Holy Spirit, submitting to His leading, so that His fragrance touches our lives and marks us as His.

Clothe ourselves in our best garments.

We are to come to Jesus clothed in the glorious garments of praise (Isa. 61:3). These garments of praise will carry us into His presence in royal style. "It is good to sing praises to our God; for it is pleasant, and praise is beautiful" (Ps. 147:1).

The Holy Spirit wants us to fall in love with Jesus! He wants to reveal to us in ever deeper ways who Jesus is. When we come to the watch, our first order of protocol is to worship the Bridegroom, to love Him and make Him the object of all our attention. Let me say again, this is our primary objective.

At the watch we aggressively steward the atmosphere of worship; we are careful not to let people's agendas, burdens or religious traditions overwhelm or remodel what God has revealed to us. Jesus says, "I love you. I want to reveal Myself to you. I want My people to see Me and love Me. Let's have a date." We steward our date time as a farmer stewards a garden, weeding it and caring for it.

The atmosphere is so precious, even angels want to join us! A guest speaker told what he saw one night during a conference we had:

> Right at the height of the worship I was looking at the altar, and it was as if an angel came down to join the worship team just for half a minute or a minute. He sounded a wind instrument that

had the cleanest, purest sound. It went all through my being. I know during the old days there were heavenly choirs. We want that to come again. We want to welcome the ministering spirits. I sense that someone from heaven's orchestra came to minister to us. It has changed my life.

The following morning the guest speakers found a reed from a wind instrument on the floor near the worship instruments on stage. No one on the worship team was playing a wind instrument! In fact, they didn't even have any wind instruments with them. The reed was given to the guest speaker who saw the angel.

In this atmosphere of worship, we tell Jesus, "Lord, You're beautiful! You're wonderful! I love You, Lord. I'm here to spend the night at Your feet, to spend all night in Your presence. I'm here to listen to Your voice. Nothing is more important to me at this minute than being with You. Tell me what to do, and I will do it. I am here to listen to Your heartbeat and learn what is on Your heart. I want to be one with You."

How many times have you been in church and wished the worship could just go on and on because it was so wonderful? But after a time, you had to go on with the announcements and the message. In regular services, these things need to be done. Preaching the Word is important, and God confirms His Word with signs and wonders. But the worship in those services is often just an appetizer, an hors d'oeuvre. On watch night, however, we get a feast. We get to worship for hours, just loving on Jesus.

One night in August 1997 we received two separate words regarding this intimacy of worship. Both concerned the woman who broke the alabaster jar of costly fragrant oil and anointed Jesus with it (Matt. 26:7). Like the woman, we lavishly pour upon the head of Jesus the oil of our praises. That night, the Lord showed us that our praise and worship were received by Him and recorded in the heavenlies as a memorial to our adoration of Him.

We are a royal priesthood. We are to offer spiritual sacrifices, which include worship and praise, two of the many aspects of prayer.

A NEW DIMENSION OF PRAYER

OUR EXPERIENCE WITH the watch has taken us into a new dimension of communion with the Lord that has redefined much of what we understood about prayer. In this hour the Holy Spirit is drawing us into more intimate fellowship with God, waiting for us to take the bold initiative of spending the night at His feet in demonstration of the intensity of our desire for Him. When we come to spend the night at His feet, He awakens to us as Boaz did; He blesses us and gives us instructions. And the whole experience becomes prayer.

To the natural man, the idea of just being with Jesus can seem like a waste of time. For those of us who like to be *doing* something all the time, just *being* seems unnatural. Our religious training says that we'd better get into some serious prayer, some real intercession. We'd better start praying for people who need help, for situations that we know need God's intervention. We are here to pray, so let's do it.

The idea of prayer always connotes, "do, do, do!" But the watch has been "be, be, be." Jesus is reminding us, "My yoke is easy and My burden is light" (Matt. 11:30). Prayer as being is something you absorb, not dissect, because it's all about the living presence of the Lord.

But the secret is that, though we're not doing anything "super-spiritual," God still accomplishes His purposes through us. We may spend much more time worshiping Him and telling Him how much we love Him than in what we normally call prayer. We've discovered that we may spend two hours kissing His feet and adoring Him, and two minutes saying, "By the way, Lord, we'd love for you to take care of this problem." But that can accomplish more than if we'd been making lists and crying before Him for hours.

The Lord is not in a hurry when we go on a date with Him during the watch. Each date, each watch, has its own personality. Often, it's joyful. But the Lord, the Bridegroom, sets the agenda. Just as Naomi assured Ruth, "He will tell you what to do," so we too are assured that when we come into God's presence, He will tell us what to do. We do not tell our Date what to do; He leads us. That's part of the secret, the difference between the old idea of intercession and watching.

When we are open to the Holy Spirit, being humbled by Him, just adoring the Lord Jesus, then out of that communion, all other things follow. When quality time is given to praise, worship and thanksgiving, the rest flows. We enthrone God on the praises of His people, and there is an atmosphere of victory, healing, deliverance, salvation and redemption.

We don't have to travail in a soulish way, making a lot of sound and fury, but producing very little. He leads by the Holy Spirit and provides insight, instruction, information, interpretation and intelligence regarding the enemy's plans. When He says so, we take authority; we bind; we pray for healing and anoint people with oil.

Are we interceding in the watch? Yes. We are putting our bodies, emotions, minds, creative abilities and voices—ourselves—in the breach, on the wall. We're presenting ourselves in that place we're calling the watch in the same way that a watchman takes his post on the wall—in the breach as an intercessor between God's purposes and the condition of earth. We are interceding by being there, just as a watchman is working when he walks the walls. When we watch, we are walking the walls, being alert in the anointing, being open and available, communing with the Lord. Then, when the Lord instructs, we act.

If God gives us scriptures to proclaim or songs to sing or a prayer to pray, that's what we do. Or He may say, "Just be with Me. Let's just enjoy one another tonight. I will take care of all the business." Then that's what we do. Either way, we are praying, and He is answering.

Relationship between the Lord and us is most important. Relationship precedes intercession. Jesus abided in constant relationship with His Father; He was jealous for that relationship, often choosing time with His Father over sleep, food and comfort, as we have seen. When Jesus went to Lazarus's tomb, He acknowledged His living and active relationship with His Father:

> Father, I thank You that You have heard Me. And I know that
> You always hear Me, but because of the people who are

standing by I said this, that they may believe that You sent Me.
—JOHN 11:41–42

After that, it just took a simple word to make a miracle: "Lazarus, come forth!" (v. 43). When you are abiding in the relationship, in His living presence, then you can say perhaps just one sentence over a nation, over a situation, and it's done. No lengthy travail, just the power that comes with the presence of God.

> If you abide in Me, and My words abide in you, you will ask what you desire, and it shall be done for you.
> —JOHN 15:7

This is the real secret of prayer: Once we are in His presence, we have what we desire because our will becomes lost in the will of the Lord. We automatically pray the prayers that are on His heart. Just one word from Him, and it is done. It may not even require a word. That level of spiritual intimacy can bring heaven alongside. We become caught up in our time with the Lord, just as the lovers portrayed in the Song of Solomon. "You have ravished my heart, my sister, my spouse; you have ravished my heart with one look of your eyes" (Song of Sol. 4:9). How can the Bridegroom withhold any good thing from the bride He loves?

So, effective prayer, which we all desire so fervently, is *being,* not *doing.* Otherwise, it is just religious work in which people get worn out and disappointed; if they don't see their prayers answered, they get frustrated and angry. That's not being led by the river of the Holy Ghost. The new dimension to prayer that God is showing us through the watch is the key to intercession: being with Him.

INTIMACY WITH GOD

THERE IS A knowing, an intimacy of communion, that others cannot understand who have not entered the bridal chamber with Him. The word the Lord has given to us is, "Come into My chamber!" The

Holy Spirit is inviting us to come away with Him, into His secret chamber, where we will yield to His whispers and touch the divine. There, He also touches us, and we are transformed.

The intimacy between a husband and a wife is a very sensitive time. It is wonderful. You feel gushy and romantic. The atmosphere is full. At that time, when your bridegroom feels romantic toward you, you do not turn to him and say, "Mow the lawn, and by the way, you haven't fixed the leaky faucet yet." That is the quickest way to kill romance, isn't it? In the same manner, we should just enjoy the intimacy with the Lord. Later on, we can say, "I have a list for You here," but not then.

Some passages from the Song of Solomon reveal the Lord as the passionate Lover enraptured with the beauty of His bride:

> Rise up, my love, my fair one, and come away.... Let me see your face, let me hear your voice; for your voice is sweet, and your face is lovely.
> —SONG OF SOLOMON 2:10, 14

> You have ravished my heart with one look from your eyes.
> —SONG OF SOLOMON 4:9

> I am my beloved's, and my beloved is mine.
> —SONG OF SOLOMON 6:3

> Let him kiss me with the kisses of his mouth—for your love is better than wine.
> —SONG OF SOLOMON 1:2

This is no longer ancient Hebrew poetry to us; we are living it. During our watch at the time of Pentecost in 1996, it was raining outside. The wind had blown earlier in the watch, then all the storm activity died down.

Around 3:30 in the morning, I declared, "We welcome the fire! Thank You for Your refreshing wind!" Suddenly a cool wind rushed through the building, even though it was no longer storming outside.

All the watchmen responded with shouting and cheers of excitement as the Lord "kissed us" with the wind. Prophetic songs of praise and adoration came forth as the breeze continued to refresh us. Soon the wonderful fragrance of the Lord's presence accompanied the breeze. Many people wept for joy and sang in the Spirit.

Bonnie recalled being "kissed" by the Lord in the breeze in Jerusalem some years ago, but this was the only other time she experienced this supernatural wind. Another watchman said, "The gentle breeze seemed to linger upon the skin of my cheeks. I began to cry, as did everyone else. I believe the reason the breeze seemed to linger on our faces was that the Lord Himself had come and planted a kiss on each of our cheeks." Another watchman described it like this:

> From the back of the church came a breeze, very gently and sweetly blowing on us. Suddenly, the Lord was there, and He brushed a kiss across my lips. It felt like a tender breeze. He said, "Everyone thinks I'll be in a white gown with a towel draped over My arm to serve them at our marriage supper—not so!"
>
> Sparkles of color seemed to fly around me and He said, "This is how it will be." He reached out His hand and grabbed the colors, like in a rainbow, and shook them like a matador's cape and began to twirl it about Him. He threw the rainbow cloth around me and drew me into the folds of His royal blue garment. From this moment on, I could dwell close to Him and know His heart.

Our Kinsman-Redeemer is spreading His mantle over us, protecting and including us, taking us into His heart. And we are falling in love with Jesus at the watch.

Jesus clearly stated that people in the last day will say to Him, "'Lord, Lord, have we not prophesied in Your name, cast out demons in Your name, and done many wonders in your name?' And then I will declare to them, 'I never knew you; depart from Me, you who practice lawlessness!'" (Matt. 7:22–23).

We believe Jesus is saying to them, "We never communed. We never came together in intimacy, where I could birth in you my purposes and bring them to bear. You delighted in My gifts, but not in Me."

God is calling us into intimate communion with Him, so that when we see Him and He sees us, He will know us and we will know Him, because we have known Him in the place of prayer. Then He will say, "Well done, good and faithful servant... Enter into the joy of your lord" (Matt. 25:21).

The watch is a time of unparalleled intimacy with the Lord.

THE GLORY OF HIS PRESENCE

IN THE WATCH, we enjoy Him in praise and worship for two or three hours, and then His presence comes—His glory is literally in our midst. The atmosphere becomes drenched with the glory of His holiness. His tenderness envelops us. He takes pleasure in our love.

Our definition of *glory* is the manifest, literal presence of the Lord. When His glory comes, we can experience Him with our senses; we are moved by His presence. His glory can come in many forms because He is Creator God. We have experienced everything from the actual fragrance of the Lord, to a supernatural light or cloud surrounding us, to just being emotionally or physiologically overwhelmed with a sense of peace, healing or the fear of the Lord in His holiness. The *Shekinah*—the atmosphere that immediately surrounds His Person—enters with Him when He comes into the room; it emanates from the Person of the Lord being manifest there.

God's presence is akin to light waves and sound waves—waves of energy. Every particle and every wave is permeated with His living love. If there's anything to describe the light we have seen in the watch, it's the love of God. Once you are touched by it, your heart will be consumed with total love, as if you were falling in love. The first wave is the love of God; it's overwhelming. Then immediately following is a wave of the revelation of His mercy because of His love. And then a wave of joy that comes because of the mercy.

Isaiah experienced this glory:

In the year that King Uzziah died, I saw the Lord sitting on a throne, high and lifted up, and the train of His robe filled the temple...and the house was filled with smoke.

—ISAIAH 6:1, 4

While preaching in meetings, I have seen the glory come in. Once, I was preaching in Germany, and some skinheads—neo-Nazis—were in the audience at the back of the room. I have to admit that I didn't want them there; I was thinking carnally. When the glory of the Lord entered the room, they were the first to fall and repent. I had to repent as well!

When the glory comes in my meetings, someone may be healed of cancer. I don't have to pray for them. People are just touched by His literal presence.

When the glory comes, people are saved and transformed. It's not just an assent: "OK, I'm going to take out an insurance policy so I don't go to hell." It's an absolute falling in love with the Lord Jesus and wanting nothing else but Him and to serve Him.

The glory will sustain you; the impact and wave of His presence will transform you and hold you up in the times where things are difficult. Sometimes it comes in such an overpowering way that it's very noticeable. At other times, it just oils the machinery of prayer.

King David said, "I would rather be a doorkeeper in the house of my God . . . " (Ps. 84:10). Why? He was the richest man on earth. He had everything—concubines, power, armies to command. But when he wrote this, he had come from the tabernacle where continuous worship went up (v. 1). The *Shekinah* was present. David just wanted to be around the glory.

THE GLORY SPOILS US

ONCE YOU HAVE tasted a little bit of the glory of God, you are spoiled for anything else. Like Moses, you will want more and more. Moses had been around the glory of God—in the tabernacle with the pillars of fire and smoke of the Lord's presence; on the mountain with God, physically sustained only by His glory for forty days. Yet, his great desire was for more.

Moses asked God, "Please, show me Your glory" (Exod. 33:18). The Lord put Moses in the cleft of the rock and protected him from the full vision of His glory, showing him only His back.

> Now the LORD descended in the cloud and stood with him there, and proclaimed the name of the LORD. And the LORD passed before him and proclaimed, "The LORD, the LORD God, merciful and gracious, longsuffering, and abounding in goodness and truth, keeping mercy for thousands, forgiving iniquity and transgression and sin, by no means clearing the guilty, visiting the iniquity of the fathers upon the children and the children's children to the third and the fourth generation."
>
> —EXODUS 34:5–7

When Moses descended from the mountain, the rays of light of God's glory shone from the face of Moses so that the people were afraid. He had to cover his face with a veil (vv. 29–35). These are living beams of light. That is the glory.

GOD IS REVEALED IN HIS GLORY

DID YOU NOTICE that in the glory of God's presence His attributes and His nature are revealed? We have found that the Lord will come into our presence through the many different gates of who He is.

> Lift up your heads, O you gates!
> Lift up, you everlasting doors!
> And the King of glory shall come in.
>
> —PSALM 24:9

In the Book of Joel, God came into the gate of repentance, of humbling. That also happened in 1986 in our Fort Lauderdale church. If He's coming through that doorway, that gate, then we follow Him through that gate of repentance. Sometimes He's coming through the gate of holy laughter. Or it might be the gate of deliverance or healing or peace. But whichever gate through which the King chooses to come—whichever aspect of His nature He chooses to reveal to us—we follow. We respect Him and flow with Him.

VIBRATING WITH HIS GLORY

BONNIE AND I have also discovered what we refer to as the "tuning fork principle." As we commune with Him, we join the harmonious hum of the heavenly vibration. When something is vibrating at a certain frequency, you can take a tuning fork that is not vibrating at all and put it into that atmosphere of vibration, and it will begin to vibrate to match the frequency of the atmosphere. When we get into the atmosphere of glory, we also vibrate at the frequency of the glory of God.

Conversely, when you touch the base of a vibrating tuning fork to a table top, the whole top begins to vibrate. The larger surface sends out sound waves, magnifying the sound of the tuning fork. The Watch of the Lord provides the place for us to respond corporately to the vibration of the Holy Spirit and become a sounding board for the will of the Father. As we pray and worship, we *are sending out spiritual "sound waves"* that are resonating with others of faith around the world. These *vibrations* are going to shake the very foundations of hell and usher in the revival for which we hunger.

This is how we can experience effectiveness in prayer and results in the earth. During the watch, we're on a different plane from the religious plane, from the plane of our circumstances. Instead, we get on His plane. We get quiet in our spirits, in our souls; then we let His hum and the vibration from His glory vibrate us, so that we start humming at His frequency, alert, alive and active in the anointing. Again, it's being, not doing, and it's full of His power.

THE RIVER OF THE HOLY SPIRIT

THE KEY TO this new dimension of prayer is the presence of the Holy Spirit. Without the Holy Spirit, prayer is boring! In the watch, the Holy Spirit comes as a river, a living river. In the Bible, sometimes

He comes as the wind, sometimes the fire, but in this aspect, He is the living water—the river.

Jesus told the woman at the well:

> If you knew the gift of God . . . you would have asked Him, and He would have given you living water. . . . Whoever drinks of the water that I shall give him will never thirst. But the water that I shall give him will become in him a fountain of water springing up into everlasting life.
>
> —JOHN 4:10, 14

This water is not *bios* (biological, natural life), but *zoe*—the God-kind of resurrection life, the miracle-working life. That life is in the river; it's the living water.

Jesus describes this river of the Holy Spirit, saying:

> "He who believes in Me, as the Scripture has said, out of his heart will flow rivers of living water." But He spoke this concerning the Spirit. . . .
>
> —JOHN 7:38–39

The river comes from the Lamb, from God: "And he showed me a pure river of water of life, clear as crystal, proceeding from the throne of God and of the Lamb" (Rev. 22:1). The river is pure, and it's alive. It's the person of the Holy Spirit flowing out like a river. The river has come from the presence of Jesus; it's the heart of Jesus, the Spirit of Christ. And the Father is the One who sends it.

We have found that, as we watch and pray, the river comes. We can jump into His river and let the Holy Spirit take us wherever He pleases. So when we watch, we let the river flow *in* us, and then *through* us—through our intercession and prayer. That living anointing then hits situations about which we're praying.

The river refreshes. The river brings life "wherever the river goes" (Ezek. 47:9)—the resurrection life. As we get into the river, the anointing will come into us, so we can tell dead things to live again.

Through the power of the river, we can proclaim and believe for dead marriages to come alive, dead dreams to come alive, children under the powers of death to come alive, people who are sick to be touched by the living river.

One watchman in our watch heard the Lord tell her, "You are the jars to carry the living water. Dip yourself deep into My reservoir until you're filled to overflowing. Then everywhere you go, I'll pour you out upon a thirsty world."

The very first psalm encourages us to be like trees planted by the river of water (v. 3). The trees, or people, who drink of this river have fruit in every season; their leaves will never wither but are continually green (Ezek. 47:12; Ps. 1:3). Those trees who are rooted in this river will always have life in them. Their fruit won't fail because their water flows from the presence of the living God. Their fruit will be food and their leaves medicine for the nations (Ezek. 47:12; Rev. 22:2).

The river is a fresh reminder of who the Lord is in our lives—powerful, full of life, continually flowing, never running out. We cannot drain the Lord's resources.

OBSTACLES AND THE RIVER

AS WE ARE called to the watch in our homes and in our churches, we face obstacles. Perhaps the obstacle is an unbelieving husband, rebellious children or a pastor who isn't interested in a watch in his church. Or the obstacle may be religious tradition, rebellion, fear, the power of witchcraft, poverty, disease, racism—any emotional, physical or spiritual hindrance to the flow of the Spirit, the river.

Do you know what the river of the Holy Spirit does with obstacles? Sometimes He just makes His path around them and accomplishes His purposes without ever moving the obstacles. Or, as the river deepens and the current thickens, sometimes the obstacles are lifted out of the way.

The Holy Spirit has a million different ways of doing things. He doesn't always remove the rock that would obstruct the flow; the water may just find a way around it. Sometimes the rock does have to be removed. But the river is deep enough and strong enough that the obstacle will be carried away without any problem. We don't have to bring in work crews with heavy machinery to dig up the rock, break it into little pieces and try to haul it out of the river.

Pastors, especially in counseling situations, I want you to know that the Spirit can flood a situation and bring complete restoration. The river finds a way around the obstacles. Before, we as pastors have counseled the broken, dissected the situation, tried to clean it all up, then attempted to put it back together again. But the Lord can just send His river and heal it all without all our labor.

In many local churches, the lives of pastors and associate pastors are consumed with counseling. We have found that when we welcome the river, there's almost no need for counseling. The river is the one that takes care of those needs. Therein lies the value of having regular watches at your church. How much more valuable it is for the pastor and the local church to spend time in prayer than in counseling! It's not only more practical; it is much more powerful.

POURING OUT HIS SPIRIT

WHEN WE OBEY the mandate to watch and pray, God visits with us. It remains a spontaneous living thing, even though we do it regularly as a discipline.

Bonnie and I are sounding the trumpet and gathering men and women, young and old, married and single to come down to the threshing floor once a week and spend the night at the feet of Jesus. As a result we are seeing Him fulfill His Word to the prophet Joel:

> And it shall come to pass afterward that I will pour out My Spirit on all flesh; your sons and your daughters shall prophesy, your old men shall dream dreams, your young men shall see visions. And also upon My menservants and on My maidservants I will pour out My Spirit in those days.
>
> —JOEL 2:28–29

§

The daughter of a lion is also a lion.

—Swahili axiom

Who is she who looks forth as the morning,
fair as the moon, clear as the sun,
awesome as an army with banners?

—Song of Solomon 6:10

7

The Bride
in Combat Boots

§

BONNIE AND I believe the Watch of the Lord is God's End-Time secret weapon against the powers of darkness. The watch has been kept by God for release in these last days because it is a powerful weapon against the enemy's destructive forces. We are convinced that sustained, consistent, concerted, concentrated corporate prayer will release the greatest power in the universe—and the time to do it is now.

When we came to Jesus, perhaps we just wanted a ticket out of hell. But unknowingly we signed on the dotted line, enlisting in a holy army! The body of Christ reminds me of the American movie *Private Benjamin*. The woman in the story enlisted in the army, thinking it would be like going on a cruise, and she ended up in boot camp! This "cruise" mentality also describes much of the activity and thinking of the Charismatic movement. We just want to sail along on the Bless-Me Cruise Line. But the season has changed. We must become militaristic in our devotion to come to the watch and to keep the watch.

DUAL NATURE OF THE WATCH

THE WATCH IS a time of unmatched intimacy with the Lord. But it is also a time of war. These two aspects of prayer have clearly emerged as the dual emphases of the Watch of the Lord. We have been given two images as representations of these.

First, we see the bride, beautiful in her wedding dress, who is obviously in love with her Bridegroom. Then, we see the warrior, fearlessly wielding spiritual weapons to resist the powers of darkness in the name of the Lord.

One of our prayer warriors had a vision one night as we prayed. He saw a bride adorned in full wedding raiment—but wearing combat boots! Why not? Aren't we the army of the Lord? In our case, the bride is also a warrior.

The builders of the Jerusalem wall had a trowel in one hand and a sword in the other (Neh. 4:17). They were building the wall, and they were fighting at the same time. During the watch, on one hand, there's the revelation of the real Jesus as love, promise, light and joy; on the other, there's the confrontation with the real wicked, horrible powers of darkness.

COMMISSIONED TO WAGE WAR

TODAY THE SPIRIT of the Lord is calling those who will hear to come and watch at the wall of prayer. But this is no ordinary type of prayer; it is warlike and intense in nature.

On behalf of our families, our friends, ourselves, our nation and the world, we are commissioned to take up our swords and shields and fight the enemy's hordes that are trying to destroy the church through the various breaches in the walls.

The nature of this spiritual war is clearly depicted in the Bible. We are told that the enemy of our souls is conniving and deceitful, hiding in the convenient camouflage of innocent appearances, all the while dedicated "to steal, and to kill, and to destroy" (John 10:10). He is a thief, a robber, a liar, a usurper, an accuser, a devourer, a destroyer and a tempter. And he doesn't work alone. He commands hordes of demonic spirits who seek out dark, empty places in the human soul in order to feed on the negative energy of depression, anger, bitterness and unbelief.

Thus, our enemies are not "flesh and blood, but . . . principalities . . . powers . . . the rulers of the darkness of this age . . . spiritual hosts of wickedness in the heavenly places" (Eph. 6:12). Throughout history we have seen the trail of these forces at work. Religious wars. Racial discrimination. Nazi concentration camps. Siberian slave labor camps. Insurrection. Revolution. Repression. Persecution. Violence. Genocide. In every generation, spiritual wickedness seeks to control thought patterns through vain and worthless philosophies, intellectual elitism, mass communication and self-serving leaders.

Everywhere we look, we see individuals caught in the various webs of addictions, violence, divorce, inner turmoil, immorality, witchcraft and spiritual confusion. The destruction spreads like a virus in society, leaving behind a wake of anger, fear and despair. The result is moral breakdown and spiritual anarchy.

LIBERATION FROM THE POWERS OF DARKNESS

AS NEVER BEFORE, the world needs liberation from these wicked spiritual forces. The enemy must be dislodged and his strongholds torn down. So God is recruiting an army—trained warriors who will establish a beachhead through intercession so that the rest of the troops that follow can go in with the Word of God and dispel the kingdom of darkness.

The Spirit of the Lord is searching for soldiers of prayer who will not break rank, become intimidated, flee the scene of battle or change course without orders from the Captain of the Host. Jesus is looking for mature, steadfast soldiers who will fight as one mighty unit, fixing their focus on bringing damage to the enemy, rather than on attacking one another.

As the enemy attacks, he tries to create fear in us and isolate us from one another. He is a defeated foe and yet, he will try to put terror in us. But our Commander in Chief, Jesus Christ, is by our side. We may be scared, but we still stand there with our swords and do battle. As we build up our spiritual muscles—and are built up in our most holy faith through prayer and fasting, proclaiming the Word and serving the Lord in obedience—courage, tenacity and the fear of the Lord will strengthen us in battle and grow us up in the fullness of the character of Christ.

One of our watchmen saw this image one watch night:

> I saw us, God's army, lined up in rows, ready for inspection. As we stood, the Lord walked through the aisles, generally pleased, although correcting things here and there. I had the sense that it was the final inspection before going out to battle. Then I noticed that we weren't wearing dress uniforms, as we normally would be at an inspection. We were wearing camouflage fatigues, boots and all.
>
> The interesting part was our weaponry—some had rams' horns, some drums, some stringed instruments (representing praise and worship). All had swords; all had the Word in our backpacks. Each had full backpacks—filled with those things the Lord knew each would need for the role he or she would carry out. We had received the training we needed to use what we had. Everyone's fatigues were padded at the knees, representing the prayer and intercession all needed to be a part of.

The watch is a practical preparational tool for the *steeling* of the church for the battle.

ANGEL BACKUP

AS WE GO into battle during the Watch of the Lord, we have "angel backup." While driving to the watch one night, one of our watchmen saw a large angel appear before him. His figure reached into the heavens and in his hand he held a large sword. As he stood, he took the sword and raised it above his head as if to declare war. The watchman knew that this angel was the angel of the watch. He was here to do battle on our behalf. He had strategic plans of war.

The forces of heaven are waiting for the children of God to send them on assignment. What we loose on earth is loosed in heaven. So on Friday nights as we go to war, we loose the angels of God to go forth and fight the powers of darkness.

We can release the angels to rush to the scenes of crimes, stop child abuse, encounter the suicidal, protect missionaries and Christian workers, intercept terrorist bombs and more. As we watch, the angels will come to assist us in accomplishing the purposes of God.

They are awesome in their power and majesty because they come from the presence of God. On several occasions in my ministry, when an angel has come, there were distinct results. On occasion, delight and terror have joined together in my heart when the angel manifested an aspect of his awesome presence. Electrical lights have burned out, masses of people have fallen simultaneously, and instant healings and deliverances have taken place.

During one watch, a family came who had driven over ten hours from Alabama just to bring their mother who was terminally ill with stomach cancer. She had been told that she had about three weeks to live.

That evening the river of praise was strong, and we kept flowing in it. At 1:00 A.M. the woman with cancer appeared fatigued. The adult children kept looking inquiringly at me, wondering when I would pray for their mother. We kept worshiping until 2 A.M., then 3 A.M. Sometime in that hour I saw the angel of God enter the barn. This angel had bright rainbow hues emanating from its body. I knew the angel had brought healing from the throne room (Rev. 4:3; 10:1). I smiled at the children, saying, "Now we will pray for your mom."

During the next week we received a call from the family saying that the doctors could no longer find the cancer in their mom. In fact, we found out that the morning after the angel appeared, she had a meal of gravy, potatoes, sausage and biscuits, and she felt fine.

Not only was she free of cancer, but her diabetes and high blood pressure had also been turned around.

The subject of angels should be approached with awe and respect. When they come, they mean business. They come to overcome the strategies of Satan and his demonic army. Sometimes they remove hindrances the devil has put in front of believers. It is important that as they come to assist us, we obey the word they bring.

I am comforted to know that these awesome holy beings are given by God to assist us. A watchman from Georgia reported that during one watch she saw "our sanctuary filled with warrior angels—white robes, swords and huge wings. They were just standing, sent to protect us."

"Are they not all ministering spirits sent forth to minister for those who will inherit salvation?" (Heb. 1:14). And they are appointed to be guardians over our children: "Take heed that you do not despise one of these little ones, for I say to you that in heaven their angels always see the face of My Father who is in heaven" (Matt. 18:10).

Ask for their assistance when you watch and pray. Remember, there are more with us than are with the army of darkness! When the Syrian armies came against Israel, they surrounded the city of Dothan where Elisha lived. Elisha's servant was terrified when he saw the horses and chariots all around them. But Elisha said:

> "Do not fear, for those who are with us are more than those who are with them." And Elisha prayed, and said, "LORD, I pray, open his eyes that he may see." Then the LORD opened the eyes of the young man, and he saw. And behold, the mountain was full of horses and chariots of fire all around Elisha.
>
> —2 KINGS 6:16–17

Angels seem to be more activated since we started to watch and pray consistently. When the angels are finished with their assignments, they disappear. Don't focus on the angel, but exalt the Lord God who sent the angel.

114

SPIRITUAL WEAPONS FOR A SPIRITUAL BATTLE

WHEN WE VIEW the forces of evil at work in our world, our enemy appears formidable. Our Lord, however, has equipped us for the battle. He is our victorious Captain, the One who will lead us in the fight. He has provided mighty weapons that will always triumph over the powers of darkness. But these weapons, like Gideon's, are not what one would expect.

> The weapons of our warfare are not carnal but mighty in God for pulling down strongholds, casting down arguments and every high thing that exalts itself against the knowledge of God, bringing every thought into captivity to the obedience of Christ.
> —2 CORINTHIANS 10:4–5

Since our warfare is not in the physical realm, neither are our weapons. We are wrestling against spiritual forces, demonic forces, demonic powers and wickedness that hold reign in high places (Eph. 6:12). We will not pull down strongholds over the various regions around the world via letter-writing campaigns, marches or church programs. We need supernatural artillery, and God has provided an arsenal of firepower in order to get us through every conceivable conflict. Only prayer can span the globe and travel great distances in the spirit, accomplishing God's purposes and carrying out His plans.

These supernatural weapons available to us for use in prayer and intercession include:

- *Protective armor.* In Ephesians 6:4–18, we find the covering that gives us safety in the heat of battle: truth, righteousness, salvation, readiness to run with the gospel of peace and the shield of faith. Through these articles of protection we are covered from head to foot!

- *The sword of the Spirit.* The Word of God is our chief weapon. Jesus wielded this weapon against Satan in the

115

wilderness temptation. (See Luke 4:1–13.) If it worked for Jesus, it will work for us! Since Satan operates in the realm of lies and deceit, he cannot stand the truth of God's Word. Truth is the laser light that penetrates demonic deception and exposes the work of Satan for what it is.

- *Praying in the Spirit.* The devil and the flesh have resisted prayer in the lives of believers, because prayer is the "atomic bomb" that can overcome all the spiritual hosts of wickedness. When we are caught up in mental conflict over the impossibility of our position, the secret to victory is praying in the Holy Ghost—in tongues. The answer isn't in trying to figure out a strategy or to focus on past failures. We are to pray in the Spirit—with a vengeance!

  When we come to a brick wall and need divine guidance, we pray in the Spirit. In areas we have struggled to overcome and yet seem powerless, the answer is, again, pray in the Spirit! The beauty of praying in tongues (our "prayer language") is that this mode of prayer bypasses our mental confusion and reasoning and becomes a direct hotline to heaven. The Holy Spirit is helping our weaknesses, and He is praying through us the perfect prayer on our behalf. (See Romans 8:26–27.)

  Powerful prayer in tongues not only leaves a tremendous spiritual deposit in the lives of those who pray, but praying in one's heavenly language can also impact the nations and change global destinies. Why? Because these prayers are directly led by the outpouring of the Holy Spirit, who always knows the perfect prayer.

- *Worship and praise.* What we do in the watch may seem powerless; we simply come together to love the Lord and sing praises to Him. What could be more innocent? But we are actually delivering a lethal blow to the enemy as we do this. Our praise, ascending to the Lord, scatters the forces of darkness and releases the light and glory of God's presence. God literally indwells (inhabits), rides upon and clothes Himself in the praises of His people. (See Psalm 22:3.)

Worship is far from idle activity. It confuses the enemy. It breaks through the clouds of demons and scatters them. Praise creates a vibration that brings pain to the devil's ears. Praise breaks bondages in our own spirits, liberating more worship and praise.

• *Binding the strongman.* The evil one, whom Jesus referred to as "the strongman," can only maintain his power until one stronger comes. (See Matthew 12:25–29 and Mark 3:22–27.) Through His victory on the cross, Jesus has bound the strongman. In Jesus' name, we can take the spoils of battle, stealing back what the enemy has stolen and releasing captives from the dungeons of darkness and destruction.

• *Resisting the devil.* The watchman has the right to challenge all who approach him while he is on duty. Satan has no "pass" to enter. When we resist him, he must flee! (See James 4:7.)

• *Gifts of the Spirit.* The gifts of the Spirit are part of our battle gear. (See 1 Corinthians 12:4–11.) Through the supernatural working of the Holy Spirit, we are able to discern the spirits of darkness at work in order to bring their deception into the open. The Holy Spirit gives special "intelligence" through words of knowledge, unique strategies through words of wisdom. The gift of faith enables us to see the victory before the fact and to press in to claim rightfully what belongs to the people of God.

The gifts of the Spirit are not toys for the spiritual playpen; they are weapons for the battlefield. When we use them as God intended, we will see God's power at work in situations previously considered hopeless. Healing, deliverance and miracles—all flow from the anointing of the Holy Spirit as we step into the arena of prayer.

- *The word of our testimony.* Another key to victory in prayer is the bold declaration of what God has already done. (See Revelation 12:11.) Faith is strengthened as we remind ourselves (and Satan) of past victories, hailing the God who is ever the same—yesterday, today and forever—as the source of that victory.

- *Unity (agreement).* An army must move as one single unit in order to be effective. When God's people stand shoulder to shoulder, shields overlapping, bound together in total agreement, there can be no defeat! It only takes two or three to bring about the power of agreement.

- *The blood of Jesus.* When face to face with demonic powers, a watchman must know the source of divine authority in order to stand in absolute assurance of victory.

    During a crusade in Africa, the Lord gave me a revelation of the power of His blood over demonic forces. I saw witch doctors in the crowd and knew their threat was real and that they had the power to command death. I also knew that demon spirits could manifest themselves in terrifying ways, causing people to fall on the floor, hissing and writhing like snakes. It was in this context that the Lord spoke to me: "One drop of the blood of Jesus can destroy the kingdom of Satan." Every demon must bow to the authority of the blood of Jesus Christ. Demons and their manifestations are no problem for true believers who understand the overcoming power of the blood of Jesus.

UNTIL WE SEE RESULTS

WE HAVE NOTICED that Christians are looking for power manifestations—signs and wonders—to confirm their Christian experience. We firmly believe, both from experience and from what the Bible indicates, that one of the major ingredients of the apostolic church that moves in signs and wonders is the foundation of perseverance. The watch is a practical threshing floor, a practical gym, so to speak—a place to build an internal place that God can endow with apostolic signs and wonders.

We just don't keep the watch for a week, then drop out. We believe that the watch is more of a marathon than a sprint. As soldiers in God's army, we need to be regular and faithful to the watch. Even when our souls balk, we need to take our places on the wall. As watchmen, we are faithful to stay on the wall until we see the results manifested.

> I have set watchmen on your walls, O Jerusalem; they shall never hold their peace day or night. You who make mention of the LORD, do not keep silent, and give Him no rest *till* He establishes and *till* He makes Jerusalem a praise in the earth.
> —ISAIAH 62:6–7, EMPHASIS ADDED

Your Jerusalem may be your marriage, your children, your circumstances. Don't give up! Don't quit until the kingdom of God is established in that situation. Some things we may not see until Jesus comes. That's why we need to continue the watch.

The Lord can give some R and R occasionally, some rest and relaxation, but that doesn't mean we step out of it permanently. There may be seasons where the Lord will say, "You can take a rest for two weeks." But we need to go back. That's a job description for a watchman. There's the willingness to persevere. In our own experience, we have found that disciplining ourselves to go down to the Lord's threshing floor of the watch has been a huge blessing.

The watch is military discipline, even though we do not follow a rigid schedule. Watchmen are soldiers on duty, praying over their city, binding the strongman and deactivating the forces of evil. This makes the devil very unhappy, but for us it is fun because we know that we are taking back the land and, in the process, developing "spiritual muscles" via our prayers. We are spending time with the Lord, and as a result, we are being changed.

During the watch we fast from food and sleep in order to spend time with the Lord. The discipline for preparing and doing battle is humbling ourselves through prayer and fasting, saying, "Lord, I don't have the answers, but You do." Fasting from sleep or food is the scriptural way of saying, "God, You are our answer." One of the greatest stumbling blocks to achieving victory is a spirit of pride. It is a great enemy to the church. We smite the power of pride through practicing humility.

At first, your body may react to the watch as it does to a fast. When you fast and miss your first meal, your body says, "I'm dying here." You have to tell your body, "Shut up! We are going to fast."

In the same way, as you start fasting from sleep, your body says, "Hey, I am going to give you a headache if you don't go to sleep." You just have to answer, "Hush! We are going to watch."

The watch is the channel through which God speaks to us about the needs of the world. It is also the vehicle He uses to commission us to do the work. The anointing comes upon us—the army of the Lord—and the work of the healing of the nations begins to take shape as we fulfill the commission to ministry as detailed in Luke 4:

> The Spirit of the LORD is upon Me, because He has anointed Me to preach the gospel to the poor; He has sent Me to heal the brokenhearted, to proclaim liberty to the captives and recovery of sight to the blind, to set at liberty those who are oppressed; to preach the acceptable year of the LORD.
>
> —LUKE 4:18–19

ARMED AND DANGEROUS

WE CAN PICTURE the Bridegroom standing back in admiration of His bride. He sees her form, outlined beneath her wedding veil, and her every feature wins His approval. "Your neck is like the tower of David, built for an armory, on which hang a thousand bucklers, all shields of mighty men" (Song of Sol. 4:4).

As the world stares in wonder, the Bridegroom declares, "Who is she who looks forth as the morning, fair as the moon, clear as the sun, awesome as an army with banners?" (Song of Sol. 6:10). Looking closer, we see the one-word insignia on those banners: LOVE.

The bride is marching under a standard that the world can never understand. Her Bridegroom—the King's cause and the reason for the conflict since the foundations of the world—is exemplified in that single word. Only His love will release captives and plant His royal seal of redemption on their foreheads. The battle is a war of liberation worldwide, and the army of the Lord is marching under that banner of love to bring deliverance, healing and hope to the nations.

Yes, there are strongholds, and the enemy is entrenched. The darkness is thick, but the enemy has cause to beware: The warrior-bride is coming, dressed in combat boots. She is armed and dangerous, ready to stand until His will is done on earth as it is in heaven.

> The kingdoms of this world have become the kingdoms of our Lord and of His Christ, and He shall reign forever and ever!
> —REVELATION 11:15

§

Call to Me,
and I will answer you,
and show you great and mighty things,
which you do not know.

———

—Jeremiah 33:3

Prophetic Watchmen

BONNIE AND I love to read and, like so many others, we have found the story of the maiden voyage of the *Titanic* fascinating. One of the best accounts of this terrible sea disaster is *The Titanic Sinks* by Thomas Conklin.[1] We believe the sinking of the *Titanic* to be a contemporary prophetic parable for the church in this hour.

The *Titanic* struck the iceberg at 11:40 P.M. That's where many eschatologists agree that we are right now on God's prophetic time clock—about twenty minutes before spiritual "midnight," when the Lord will return, just as promised in Scripture.

The "unsinkable" *Titanic,* elaborately outfitted with the best of everything money could buy, was a picture of elegance, elitism and state-of-the-art engineering. Aboard this behemoth was a cross-section of all society: the very poor were cramped together in its third-class belly; the middle-class working people in second-class steerage cabins; and the wealthiest families of Europe and America in first-class suites.

Every whim of the wealthy and elite had been anticipated and provided for. Live palm trees in Oriental pots decorated the private terraces that spanned the first-class decks, and the first-class passengers dined at tables set with the best china, crystal and silver. Children of the rich passengers were amused by the rocking horses that dotted the deck, or they could play shipboard games. There were indoor swimming pools, European spa facilities, gaming courts, afternoon teas, cigars and brandy in the library for the men after the elaborate, multicourse dinner and dancing to the ship's orchestra.

A well-publicized feature of this fabulous vessel was the latest technology of the day. The wireless operators stayed busy at their stations, accepting congratulations and well-wishes from land for the first-class passengers, who responded back with urgent messages of both a social and business nature. And the business being conducted was nothing less than high-level business, since the *Titanic's* passenger list featured some of the world's most noteworthy millionaires—John Jacob Astor, Levi Strauss and Benjamin Guggenheim.

Aboard the *Titanic* for her maiden voyage was a representation of the very finest the world had to offer in the year 1912—the best, the brightest, the richest, the most talented, the most clever, the most privileged. Yet all those hopes, dreams and resources were about to be plunged to the bottom of the frozen North Atlantic. Only God Himself knew that, as the ship left the port at Southampton, England, more than half of all those aboard had just a few more days to live. Of the sixteen hundred-plus passengers, less than seven hundred survived one of history's most infamous disasters at sea.

PEERING INTO THE NIGHT

ON THAT TRAGIC night, the *Titanic's* two watchmen, Frederick Fleet and Reginald Lee, were doing their jobs up in the crows' nest. As the people were eating, drinking and dancing inside the ship's grand salons, Fleet and Lee, exposed to the cold and the elements, kept a watch out for any icebergs. But they did not have the necessary equipment—binoculars. These were not supplied.

The collision with the iceberg might have been prevented simply had these watchmen been equipped with the binoculars they needed in order to see farther into the night. One pair of binoculars may have saved the *Titanic*.

As it turned out, the ship was so close to the iceberg field that, by the time it could be seen with the naked eye, not even the first mate's hasty command—"Turn around and slow"—was enough to avoid collision. The ship hit and slid its length against the lethal black ice—the kind that is mostly underwater and hidden from surface view.

PROPHETIC WATCHMEN

HOW CAN WE draw a parallel between the *Titanic's* watchmen and those of us called to watch on the wall in prayer? Although Fleet's and Lee's jobs seemed of little importance in comparison to the officers who outranked them, the fates of officers and passengers alike turned out to be in their hands. Their jobs were cold and lonely, but they were the first to spot the iceberg and the first to warn of the impending danger.

The job of prophetic intercessors, like that of the watchmen aboard the *Titanic*, is often cold and lonely and seems of little importance, but the fates of many are in their hands. With spiritual equipment in hand, the prophetic watchman looks out ahead of the rest and reports back so any threat can be diverted and the course safely navigated.

However, spiritual watchmen don't only look ahead. The watchmen on the wall of prayer are also seeking God Himself—His company, His face. So the watchmen turn their faces upward as well, looking at the Lord. Supernatural discernment comes from looking at the Lord.

THE PROPHETIC INTERCESSOR IN THE WATCH

THROUGHOUT THE BIBLE we notice God using signs, visual images, parables and actions to communicate His Word. This phenomenon is being repeated today as we wait in God's presence. Watchmen receive insights during the watch, and before we all leave, we give opportunity for our watchmen to share what they've observed while looking ahead or looking up. What emerges is a corporate picture of what God is trying to say to us.

Often several individuals will be given a piece of the prophetic puzzle. When put together, all the pieces fit together to confirm the whole. Or several watchmen will receive similar words, such as directives to fast or words of encouragement regarding faith or provision. Sometimes several people in different watches receive impressions or specific words about the same symbol, such as water, fire, earthquakes, the lion, the army—even alligators! The separate words can reveal different aspects of something the Lord is saying to us.

At the beginning of one watch, when it was still held in our barn, three people saw through the open barn doors an eagle circling low in the sky. It descended and perched on a fence outside the barn and sat for a while, very still, as if observing.

During that watch, one person received a vision of a huge eagle with gold and white feathers that swooped in through the barn doors with eyes set on everyone—with the ability to see deeply in the Spirit. Another watchman had the impression that the river of worship was a river of air currents, rather than a river of living water. On these air currents eagles sent by the Lord flew into the barn. The eagles soared over everyone, seeking out the snakes, snares and bondages that were wrapped around people's feet. As the eagles spied the bondages, they swooped down and with their sharp beaks tore them from the people. They carried away the bondages, thereby freeing the people.

Prophetic intercession may come to our musicians, prompting spontaneous songs that are brand-new—songs that have never been sung before, elevating the Word of God to new heights. We see from the psalms that David often sang a new song to God. "He has put a new song in my mouth" (Ps. 40:3).

Songs also flow after the reading of a passage of Scripture, with the text itself providing the lyrics. In essence, these songs are an interpretation of Scripture, bringing it into the moment and capturing its meaning in a fresh new way.

Movement can also be initiated by the Holy Spirit. A dance may express a unique burden through its movements. Or a "Jericho march" may capture the Lord's desire for us to "possess the land" in determined intercession. Or the waving of a banner may declare our corporate allegiance to the Lord and His purposes.

Each revelation, vision or prophetic interpretation must align with God's written Word. What never ceases to amaze Bonnie and me is how the Holy Spirit continually sheds fresh light on the Word of God, bringing to it a fresh relevance—full of power and application for today. For instance, after we'd been doing the watch corporately for a while, we suddenly started seeing all the revelation and life in Scripture on the word *watch.* It was very encouraging to see the centrality and power of watching as a tool for salvation, intervention and victory in every circumstance and season. The Holy Spirit still points out new aspects of the watch in Scripture that we realize we are experiencing today as we keep the watch.

The people receiving the true prophetic stream are also the people who are involved in consistent intercession following the living word of the Lord—what He is saying to us at that moment. Those who pay the price as watchmen will also be rewarded with the spirit of revelation to know the times and the seasons in which we live and how to respond and influence others.

This is continually taught by Jesus in every statement He makes about "watching" as the end of the age approaches. He assures the vigilant ones they will not be unaware or in the dark about what hour it is and what they should do in relation to the events of the end of the age. But Paul assures the believers, "But you, brethren, are not in darkness, so that this Day should overtake you as a thief. You are all sons of light and sons of the day. We are not of the night nor of darkness. Therefore let us not sleep, as others do, but let us watch and be sober" (1 Thess. 5:4–6).

In order to have the true spirit of Christ, which is discerning and responding to particular events as He would, we must do what Jesus did: spend time with the Father watching and communing in prayer, absorbing the heart and Spirit of the Father.

PRAYING WITH PROPHETIC INSIGHT

THE WATCH OF the Lord has already yielded much fruit for the kingdom of God. We know that from the many testimonies we have received from all parts of the globe, from people who have shared how God has met needs, performed miracles and answered prayers.

But another incredible thing happens when watchmen gather to pray. We step into the river of the Spirit, who takes us wherever the Lord directs. In that river, revelation, insight and special knowledge flow. Because of that, we are able to pray with a kind of precision that just would not be possible without this direction and insight from God.

One watchman from Wisconsin reported that during separate watches in March and April 1998 the Lord spoke to him about violent wind storms and tornadoes coming to the Grand Rapids area. They prayed about it and asked God to preserve life. On Pentecost Sunday in May 1998, west Michigan was rocked by straight-line winds and thunderstorms reaching 130 mph. No tornadoes were reported, but 520,000 customers lost electric power, some for over a week. The storm caused over $100 million in damages. But the Lord had answered our prayers: No lives were lost. Neighbors helped neighbors. In fact, even strangers stepped in to help.

Testimonies like this are not uncommon. It's as if the Lord had been there first, seen events that were about to happen and then whispered to us, "Pray this!" As we pray according to these precise directions of the Holy Spirit, destructive events are averted and accidents are prevented.

Later, we often receive reports from other watchmen or hear news accounts about a global event, and we realize the Lord has used our directed prayer to turn events from evil to good. In His mercy, He has also sent confirmation afterward to show us yet again that His hand was directing our prayer work.

Two women from Ohio were watching together on a Friday night during the Olympic games in Atlanta in 1996. They say they were praying for many things, but the Olympic games were not really on their minds. "Suddenly the Lord gave us a vision of a bomb. We had no understanding of the meaning, so we began to pray in the Spirit. We prayed for protection and that God would foil the attempts of the enemy. We had no idea if our prayers were on target, but we continued to pray as we felt led.

"The next day we learned that a bomb had been set off at the Olympics. It showed us God wants to change destiny with prayers! Thankfully, the outcome wasn't as bad as it could have been. Praise God!"

As we discipline ourselves to be faithful to keep the watch, to stay alert, to post ourselves in position to hear from the Lord and discern Him in the watch, we receive supernatural intelligence, just as those two women received regarding the bomb. Receiving truly effective directives in prayer has been one of the living and exciting elements of the watch. Do you want to develop in your own experience the ability to really hear in the supernatural, to be involved in the Lord with it and see the results of it? Then watch and pray.

JOB DESCRIPTION OF THE PROPHETIC WATCHMAN

For thus has the Lord said to me: "Go, set a watchman, let him declare what he sees."

—ISAIAH 21:6

When disaster is coming, it is time for the watchman to get in place on the wall against the invasion. In this place God gives revelation to the watchman. It's like the sentry watching at his post night and day to observe and report any movement by the enemy in order to defend the city. The watchman is first to receive the intelligence information and sound the alarm—passing it on to the rest of the army command.

Speak to the children of your people, and say to them: "When I bring the sword upon a land, and the people of the land take a man from their territory and make him their watchman, when he sees the sword coming upon the land, if he blows the trumpet and warns the people, then whoever hears the sound of the trumpet and does not take warning, if the sword comes and takes him away, his blood shall be on his own head. . . . But he who takes warning will save his life."

—EZEKIEL 33:2–5

In these verses we have the job description of the prophetic watchman:

1. He speaks of only what he sees—only what God is showing him.

2. Rescuing sinners is his first priority. God is not willing that any should perish. The watchman is God's heart in action.

3. He remembers that the "soul" of the watchmen is tied to the people. Their blood is tied to them.

4. He accepts the responsibility that people "live and die" by the warning of the watchman.

The watchman is appointed against a time of trouble to come. As he assumes this responsibility the spirit of revelation comes on him. He is to speak only what God gives. His soul is therefore tied to the people for whom he has been appointed to stand in the gap.

MORE DISASTERS AVERTED

BONNIE AND I have documented numerous instances of the Lord's intervention in circumstances to avert disaster. He gives us His supernatural intelligence to pray about something that will happen.

In the late hours of our watch in Charlotte on Friday night, March 27, 1999, during the first couple weeks of the NATO air strikes against Yugoslavia, I had an open vision of some of the scenes from an old Spencer Tracy movie, *A Man Called Joe*. In the movie,

Spencer Tracy comes back as a guardian angel for an American pilot in World War II. I asked the Lord what this vision meant, and I sensed the Lord telling me there was a pilot who was going to be in trouble and to pray for him and the others involved.

I had members of the armed forces come up and make a circle. Then I asked several watch leaders to stand behind these people and act as "guardian angels." We prayed and appointed guardian angels for every pilot; we asked God to cover our armed forces.

We heard that a few hours later an F-117A Nighthawk stealth fighter was shot down near Belgrade. In an article from the April 6, 1999, *Albuquerque Journal,* the pilot himself testified that "the one fragment of this whole event I can't remember is pulling the (ejection seat) handles. God took my hands and pulled."[2]

The pilot hid in a culvert and witnessed flashing headlights and the barking of dogs. He said that at one time a search dog came within thirty feet of him, but he was never discovered. We believe that angels protected him.

This demonstrates how God will tell you certain things and give you supernatural knowledge. If people choose to become watchmen for their families, churches or cities, the Lord will give them vital information to utilize in prayers for their children, church or nation in the times of crisis.

Another powerful example of God speaking through a dream was the account from one of our Charlotte watchmen.

> One night I had a dream about Paris in which I saw holes around the Eiffel Tower as well as in other locations around the city. I heard a voice say, "There's a bomb hidden in one of these holes." In my dream I exclaimed, "Lord, if this bomb goes off, there are so many holes, the city could go down in no time!" I woke up shaking, filled with the knowledge that I had many friends and family there. I realized France was in danger.
>
> The next evening, September 1, 1995, I attended the Watch of the Lord and shared my dream. Another watchman jumped up and said that she had a similar dream about France earlier

that week. The watch captains concluded that we should pray for France regarding bomb threats. We proceeded to intercede on behalf of France. The Holy Spirit gave us the specific impression that there were evil plans against Jews and children.

A week later, on September 8, 1995, the *Charlotte Observer* reported this news story:

> A car bomb exploded in front of a Jewish school Thursday and injured fourteen people. A faulty school bell had kept the 700 children inside, and no one was killed. The explosion in this Lyon suburb was the sixth bombing or attempted bombing in France since late July and the first car bombing in France since 1982. Children screamed, parents wept and dense black smoke swirled in front of the school. But the words on everyone's lips were ones of relief: "It's a miracle!"
>
> The bomb was timed to go off at the moment the children were to leave school in the afternoon, but a tardy bell delayed their exit by two minutes. Police said this saved dozens of lives.[3]

The article adds, "The blast came three days after a bomb was found and defused in Paris." So bombings in two locations in France, including Paris, were averted by acting on supernatural intelligence from the Holy Spirit. Lives of young school children were spared thanks to God's supernatural intervention through dreams!

GOD SPEAKS HIS WORD—THROUGH US!

AS WE MAKE the watch a lifestyle, the Lord gives us real revelation— "the right stuff." The lives of many and the destiny of nations will eventually depend on believers watching and praying. Prayerful watching is a discipline; it is not a flippant endeavor. Serious and desperate needs are being prayed for. Because of this awesome call, we must understand that the watch, even though we have great joy and even fun in it, is absolutely life-changing and nation-building. God works His purposes through us.

When the Lord chose Jeremiah to be His prophet, He said:

> Behold, I have put My words in your mouth. See, I have this day set you over the nations and over the kingdoms, to root out and to pull down, to destroy and to throw down, to build and to plant.
> —JEREMIAH 1:9–10

In other words, in prophetic intercession God puts His words in our hearts and minds, then our mouths.

God then showed Jeremiah the branch of an almond tree. He told Jeremiah that meant "I am ready to perform My word" (v. 12). The word that the Lord gives us in prophetic intercession—through prayer, dance, words or song—He will perform. We only have to obey the direction of the Holy Spirit and do our part to affect events, people and nations.

§

I have set watchmen on your walls,
O Jerusalem; they shall never hold their
peace day or night. You who make mention
of the LORD, *do not keep silent, and give*
Him no rest till He establishes and till He makes
Jerusalem a praise in the earth.

—ISAIAH 62:6–7

9

The Watch and Israel

A T NIGHT, THE Western Wall in Jerusalem is bathed in golden light cast from six flames that burn continually in memory of the six million Jews killed during the Holocaust. If I lived there, I would probably elect to sleep during the day so I could sit up nights and watch at the Western Wall, which used to be called the Wailing Wall.

In 1995 I held my own watch night service at the Western Wall immediately following a healing service I had in Jerusalem. I sat for awhile at this famous Wall. Physically, the Wall is the remnant of the second temple built upon the foundations of Solomon's Temple. But symbolically for the Jews and Christians, it's place of communion with God—a literal illustration of the place of prayer.

The Western Wall is like an open place to heaven where man can commune with God. It represents the watch, prayer, man interceding. Jews come from all over the world to pray at the Western Wall at their high holidays or just because they are drawn there.

The Western Wall also represents the restoration of the Jews' inheritance, which has been in the hands of others for almost 2000 years. In the 1967 war, the Western Wall was taken back by the Jews as Jerusalem was repossessed. Toilets had been built over part of it. Human waste ran down onto the stones at the bottom where Solomon's Temple used to be, where the holy of holies had once been. The Western Wall was the one place, the one reminder on earth to the Jews that they were the people of God, and it had been desecrated. Having it back was a national religious and spiritual sign of God's people triumphing over their enemies.

After I sat at the Wall for a while that night, I walked over to a deep archeological pit that had been dug by workers excavating the site of Solomon's Temple. The pit was thirty to forty feet deep and was lit by work lights. I could see the foundation stones of the outer wall of Solomon's Temple, where the glory of the Lord had once been displayed. I prayed all night, inspired afresh by that glimpse of history. After a time, the Lord spoke to me: "Is there anybody who will watch with Me?" Then He said, "I'm coming earlier than you expected."

For me, being present at the Wall, watching and praying there all night, is like being at the place on earth where I can experience what it must be like to be at the throne of God—the throne as depicted in Revelation, where the golden bowls of incense—the prayers of the saints—are poured out in His presence (Rev. 8:3–5).

When I go to the Wall, the site of centuries' worth of prayers prayed and answered, I walk into an eternally holy place. I literally can feel the glorious atmosphere so charged with prayer; I experience God's divine presence enfolding me. It is like walking onto another spiritual plane—into a different realm and dimension, where time runs eternally both forward and backward. There I am, simultaneously enveloped in all three attributes of time—past, present and future—so that I am moving both forward and backward, while at the same time occupying this present reality.

I have been to the Western Wall in Jerusalem to pray every year since 1983, and each experience has been slightly different and yet curiously the same. When the sun begins to rise across the skies over Jerusalem, I am again and again awestruck at the sight. The scripture from the Book of Malachi comes to mind: "The Sun of Righteousness will rise with healing in his wings" (Mal. 4:2, NLT).

To see the sun rising over Jerusalem is a visual feast. First, from the deep darkness, you notice patches of navy blue punctuated by stars, then deep blue, then violet. Then you will see the brightest morning star. Next comes purple, followed by little specks of pink and red and reddish purple. Then this slow change quickly turns to a pink that soon lightens into day. There are few experiences more moving than seeing morning dawn over the ancient city of Jerusalem.

I WILL ARISE AT MIDNIGHT

IN THE PHYSICAL sense, as I take my place to pray at the Western Wall, a hush comes over me and settles down into my spirit as the awesome reverence of this timeless, eternal place hits me. Then slowly I get my bearings and notice my surroundings in greater detail.

Guards are standing about with their instructions to keep the peace. To the right and left I see the gnarled hands of the grandmothers and the wizened beards of the grandfathers who have come to the Wall to pray alongside the mothers and fathers and teenagers. Soldiers with their guns slung at rest across their backs have also come to pray. Heads bowed, leaning forward in prayer, sometimes rocking back and forth, those who pray appear to span the Wall like a living, wandering vine. And woven through the hundreds of hushed prayers is the gentle, persistent sound of doves cooing.

I notice the yellowed slips of paper wedged into the Wall's many cracks and crevices. These represent the many heart cries and heartbreaks of mankind left there over the centuries by those who, like me, have come to the Wall in Jerusalem for just one reason: to pray.

There is a sect of Hasidic Jews who call themselves watchmen. An old sect that has been recently revived, its members take to heart the psalmist's words: "I will arise at midnight and praise You." (See Psalm 119:62.) The sect is said to have arisen during the days of

137

David, who, they say, would be awakened by God blowing upon the strings of his harp in the middle of the night. That was his signal to arise and commune with God.

So King David was a watchman; now, following his pattern, this sect of Jews keeps watch during the night on the wall of prayer.

So must we.

WATCH ISRAEL

IT NEVER FAILS that when I go to Jerusalem, I return refreshed and re-ignited with the fire of the Holy Spirit. Going there helps me keep a finger on the prophetic pulse of what God is doing on earth.

If you want to know what God is up to, watch Israel. Watch Jerusalem. Jesus prophesied that in the last days certain things would happen, one of which is that Jerusalem would no longer be trampled by the Gentiles (Luke 21:24). Jewish government would once more be restored, He told us. That happened in 1967.

But the powers of darkness continue to vie for repossession of the land that belongs to God and His covenant people. They want to steal what belongs to God's people—to both natural Israel, the Jews, and spiritual Israel, the church of Jesus Christ. As in biblical times, we must fight against these powers of darkness if we are to keep our inheritance from falling into the enemy's hands.

So there is a call to arms against the powers of darkness, and the only ones able to heed that call and battle the enemy are those equipped to fight under God's anointing. Those who know how to use the name of Jesus, who are born again and are washed in His blood, who have power over darkness—they are the ones who can walk in God's glory and pull down the enemy's strongholds.

REMEMBER JERUSALEM

IN A JEWISH wedding, the bridegroom breaks a glass to remember the hurt of Jerusalem and her need for restoration. We must remember her, too.

Over the centuries Jerusalem has been fought over by great kingdoms in the same way jealous lovers would wrestle to win the affections of the object of their desire. Though kingdoms have longed to have her, Jerusalem belongs to God. And He shall have her for His own.

As the bride celebrates with our gracious Bridegroom, we must listen to what is on His heart. It is not enough just to enjoy the privileges of being the bride. Our hearts must be willing to share our bridal love with Jesus. In love we ask, "What is on Your heart? If Israel is on Your heart, then we will be yoked with You and share Your burden for Your people, the Jews. We will remember Jerusalem."

> Pray for the peace of Jerusalem! May they prosper who love you [the Holy City]! Peace be within your walls and prosperity within your palaces! . . . For the sake of the house of the Lord our God, I will seek, inquire for, and require your good.
> —PSALM 122:6–7, 9, AMP

Part of the mantle we have received from the Lord is the assignment to pray for the peace of Jerusalem and for the restoration of Israel according to God's purposes in the last days.

When you go to the Western Wall to pray, you are enfolded in both history and destiny as you are provoked to recall that Jews throughout history—ever since the Diaspora scattered them to the four corners of the earth in A.D. 73—have returned to the Wall from all points of the world to proclaim, *"Ba' shana ha b'ah B'yerushalayim*—Next year in Jerusalem!"

The Wall is the site of "living" stones—stones vibrantly charged with the prayers of the centuries—all proclaiming history, then mixing it with the present and the promise of the future. Hundreds of thousands of Jews have flocked there—and they still flock there—to pray and then push their written prayers on rolled-up pieces of paper into the crevices of the wall so God will not forget them.

But God spoke through an impassioned Isaiah, "How could I forget you? See, I have inscribed you on the palms of My hands."

139

(See Isaiah 49:15–16.) God has not, does not and will not forget her. We too are instructed not to forget Jerusalem. Our spiritual roots and heritage are there.

The Watch of the Lord is at all times connected with God's plan for Israel, that place of destiny where the Lord's chosen people resided. Israel is not only the place where Christ was born and ministered and died for the sins of all mankind, but the Bible clearly tells us that the site of His return is the Mount of Olives at Jerusalem. As we blow the shofar in the Watch of the Lord, and as we pray for the peace of Jerusalem, we are preparing the way for the Prince of Peace to return to earth to rule and reign from His holy city.

Israel has always wrestled for her blessing. True and lasting peace will come only when the Prince of Peace appears to establish His kingdom on the earth in Jerusalem, His chosen city. We must have a heart to pray for Jerusalem.

LOVE ME, LOVE MY FAMILY

WE PRAY FOR Israel, where so much bloodshed has taken place throughout the ages and where great battles shall surely yet be fought. We pray for Israel because God instructs us to do so in Scripture. He says, in effect, "If you love Me, love My children." With all her faults and foibles throughout time, Israel is still dear to God's heart. He loves her with an everlasting love, and a special blessing is stored up for the Gentiles who love her and learn to make prayer on her behalf a priority. Therefore, praying for Israel is a key ingredient of the Watch of the Lord.

As we are faithful to intercede for Israel, the blessing of the King of Israel shall come upon us. Many of the breakthroughs we need in our personal lives take place as we pray for God's most precious city, Jerusalem.

Bonnie and I realize how vital it is that Christians watch with—and stand with—Israel, because Israel is the key to everything that is spiritual in these last days. We know from the Word of God that Israel has always been a priority with God. And we know from the things God has told us as we have prayed that she is still so today.

TOGETHER IN CHRIST

IN 1995 AS I watched all night alone in prayer at the Western Wall, the Lord said to me, "Next year you will be joined by hundreds of people from the nations who will watch with you at the Wall and pray." Just as He said, the following year, I was joined at the Wall by five hundred watchmen from forty-seven different countries. Prayers were said in Swahili, Spanish, Hindi, Russian, Dutch, Norwegian, German and French in addition to the native languages of Samoa, Nigeria and other nations.

We sang songs together and laid hands on the Wall, petitioning the Lord to break up the fountains of the deep and release a new work that would minister His love to the Islamic nations. We could feel the power of God, like a great heavenly earthquake, literally shake the heavens as we prayed in one accord there at the Western Wall.

A week after I returned from Israel I received an e-mail about a real earthquake that occurred in the area where we had prayed. According to the Jewish Post of New York Online for October 9, 1996, "An earthquake rattled Israel this afternoon. The quake was felt throughout Israel including Jerusalem . . . The quake was rated at 6.1 on the Richter Scale."[1]

That was a sign in the natural to confirm what we had experienced in the spiritual—that God had begun a great work that night among the Islamic nations. "Show me a sign for good, that those who hate me may see it and be ashamed" (Ps. 86:17).

We hold a Western Wall watch every year at the Feast of Tabernacles. At the watch there in 1996 a woman from Georgia who went to Israel with us on our tour told of seeing a picture in her mind of the star of David as she sat praying. Superimposed over it was the symbol for atomic power—electrons circling the nucleus and making a design. She felt God telling her that He releases power on behalf of Israel when we pray for her.

Then a Messianic Jew who was with us began to pray aloud, and

141

she saw the picture again. This time, however, the atomic energy symbol was pulsating and glowing, as if it had been activated. She said, "I believe the Lord was showing me the unimaginable power of our prayers, as He is able to magnify them, when Jews and Gentiles come together in Christ, on behalf of His heart for Israel, and intercede as the 'one new man.'"

She was reminded of the scripture in Ephesians that tells of the Gentiles and Jews coming together in Christ: "For He Himself is our peace, who has made both one, and has broken down the middle wall of separation, having abolished in His flesh the enmity...so as to create in Himself one new man from the two, thus making peace" (2:14–15).

I encourage you to allow the Spirit of God to give you His prayers for Jerusalem, just as I encourage you to give the city of the Lord your prayers. You are joined together irrevocably by history and destiny, and God will bless you mightily for remembering Jerusalem each time you meet for corporate prayer.

GOD IS RESTORING ISRAEL

THE JEWS ARE a chosen people. From the time of the destruction of the temple in Jerusalem by the Romans and the Jewish Diaspora from Israel in A.D. 73, the Jews have suffered as sojourners in the earth. Outcast and unrecognized as a people, the Jews had no nation and no capital.

In 1948, the State of Israel was proclaimed by David Ben-Gurion, who became her first prime minister, and the United Nations voted to recognize the Jewish people as a nation and make the state of Israel their homeland.

Israel is a sign of restoration. I go there each year to minister in miracle services, and there I see thousands of Russian Jews who have been gathered by the Holy Spirit and returned to their homeland from the north. I also see Yemenite and Ethiopian Jews, as well as Jews from many other nations. Truly the prophetic promise contained in Jeremiah 16:14–15 is being fulfilled before our very eyes!

"Therefore, behold, the days are coming," says the LORD, "that it shall no more be said, 'The LORD lives who brought up the children of Israel from the land of Egypt,' but, 'The LORD lives who brought up the children of Israel from the land of the north and from all the lands where He had driven them.'"

—JEREMIAH 16:14–15

A MISSION TO RUSSIA

IN 1986 THE word of the Lord came to us as Bonnie and I prayed: "I want you to go to Russia. I'm giving you a word to take to these people."

I had received an invitation to go to Finland, and from Finland I went on to Russia, where I spoke to the leaders of the Refuseniks. Then I went to visit a certain rabbi. I climbed ten flights of stairs to his apartment, which was located on the outskirts of Moscow. When he opened the door, he asked, "Who are you?"

I told him my name and that I was from America. He replied, "You're the first one I've ever seen from America."

"I have a word from the Lord for you," I declared.

"The KGB is recording everything here," he revealed. "Let's go out." So we went out to a nearby park and as we walked, the rabbi again asked, "Who are you?"

"I'm just a servant of God," I replied.

He was curious about me. "You're a Jew, aren't you? You look like a Jew."

"No, I'm not a Jew."

"Where did your parents come from?"

"My parents came from India."

"There's a lost tribe of Israel in India," he insisted.

Then I gave him the word from God. "Thus saith the Lord, 'God is going to send a whirlwind of freedom. And this Communist pharaoh is going to let you go!' God is going to set you free!"

"Well," he stated, "He may release my other friends, but I will never be able to leave free."

"You are the leader, and you are going to lead this people out," I reiterated. "When the door is opened, you take the people to Israel. This is the word of the Lord."

"Well," he sighed, "that is impossible. I'm a doctor of mathematics, and I built their rockets. Now I'm a rabbi, but because I know their secrets, they will never let me go."

I repeated firmly, "This is, 'Thus saith the Lord': He is going to create a confirmation right now."

Then the rabbi said, "You speak a blessing to me as a man of God, and I will speak a blessing to you."

He spoke a rabbinical blessing upon me, and then I raised my hand and said, "O God of Abraham, Isaac and Jacob, show Yourself here." We were talking face to face in the park. When I raised my hand toward him he was slain in the Spirit, and I reached out to catch him. He exclaimed, "The pain is gone!" I discovered that he had been tortured by the KGB and was in chronic pain in his ribs. It left when God blessed him.

A couple years later in 1988 I was in Israel with my friend Ricky Skaggs. We went to the airport at three o'clock in the morning to welcome some of the first flights of Russian Jews. What a thrill that was! Although I did not see the rabbi on one of those flights, I saw the picture of him arriving in Jerusalem in the newspaper the next day. God had released him!

For decades the Marxist Communists had said, "There is no God! There is no God!" Then one day the Lord stood up and said, "There is no Communism!"

We thought it would take hundreds of years. We thought Russia was so strong and her nuclear weapons so powerful that it would take generations to overthrow Communism. Overnight God changed everything! We had taken it for granted that the Jews were held in Russian bondage, but God stood up and intervened! Now what we are seeing take place in the former Soviet Union is reformation. God is shaking the very structure of the social order and opening the door for the preaching of the gospel of Jesus Christ.

The Watch and Israel

FROM RESTORATION TO REFORMATION

THE RESTORATION OF the land of Israel is symbolic for us. God has the same desire to restore His church. We are in an historical, prophetic time, but there are certain things that we must do.

> Gird yourself with sackcloth, and lament, O priests. Wail, O ministers of the altar! Come, spend the night in sackcloth, O ministers of my God. . . . Consecrate a fast, proclaim a solemn assembly; gather the elders and all the inhabitants of the land to the house of the LORD your God, and cry out to the LORD.
>
> —JOEL 1:13–14, NAS

This is the remedy anytime we see desolation. When the enemy attacks us personally, or attacks our churches, our families or our nation, we must come to the Lord. We are to come in humility, fasting from food and sleep. We are to come corporately into the house of the Lord. And we are invited to spend the night. This is exactly what we are doing in the Watch of the Lord.

Then, in Joel 2, we see God's response:

> So rejoice, O sons of Zion, and be glad in the LORD your God. For He has given you the early rain for your vindication. And He has poured down for you the rain, the early and the latter rain as before. . . . And you shall have plenty to eat and be satisfied, and praise the name of the LORD your God, who has dealt wondrously with you; then My people will never be put to shame. Thus you will know that I am in the midst of Israel, and that I am the LORD your God and there is no other. And My people will never be put to shame.
>
> And it will come about after this that I will pour out My Spirit on all mankind; and your sons and daughters will prophesy, your old men will dream dreams, your young men will see visions. . . . I will pour out My Spirit in those days.
>
> —JOEL 2:23, 26–29, NAS

If we are faithful to the challenge of prayer, we may see reformation: a total transformation of the very structure of society, a spiritual awakening that will change history. A reformation will affect educational systems, the economic structure, healthcare issues, the moral stance in regard to crime, the media and its contents and rehabilitation programs. Reformation will root out racism and end abortion. It will affect governmental decisions and the forming of laws. It will impact the entire social order.

Following the pattern of God's restoration to His chosen people, Israel, God will do the same for His church in this hour of spiritual destiny.

THE PLACE OF DESTINY

ONCE, AS I watched in prayer at the Wall in Jerusalem, the Lord said to me, "Tell My people to remember Jerusalem. Their destiny is joined to her." So I am doing as the Lord said to do. I am telling you, "Remember Jerusalem! Your destiny is joined to her."

Unmistakably, Israel is the place of spiritual destiny for both Jews and Christians. It is where the two religions began and where our destinies will again intersect as Christ returns and puts His feet upon the Mount of Olives at Jerusalem.

PART III

§

*Come on now, all you young men
all over the world. You have not an hour to lose.
You must take your places in life's fighting line.
Don't be content with things as they are. Enter
upon your inheritance, accept your responsibilities.
Raise the glorious flags again, advance them upon
the new enemies, who constantly gather upon the
front of the human army, and have only to be
assaulted to be overthrown. Don't take no for an
answer. Never submit to failure. Do not be fobbed
off with mere personal success or acceptance. You
will make all kinds of mistakes; but as long as you
are generous and true, and also fierce, you cannot
hurt the world or even seriously distress her.*[1]

—WINSTON CHURCHILL

10

Line Upon Line, Precept Upon Precept

§

BONNIE AND I hope that by this point you are passionately ready to begin or participate in a Watch of the Lord. That's why we want to share the guidelines the Lord has taught us as we have kept watch with Him each Friday night since January 1995. We encourage you to consider these guidelines prayerfully in order to be blessed with a fuller release of the Holy Spirit during any sort of watch night service you may implement.

But more importantly, we encourage you to seek the Lord's counsel as to how and when to apply any of these ideas, since the Lord, as Captain of the Host of Heaven, is the one who is ultimately in charge of our watch activities.

While these are not hard-and-fast rules that must be kept or else, they are principles that work, and we believe they will help you. The model for the watch that the Lord has given us is very palatable, even to Westerners. It can flow in every culture, yet it gives each group the liberty to develop its own identity.

Every watch is different, and every date with Jesus is distinct. The watch in Richmond, Virginia, is not going to be the same as our watch in Charlotte. The watch in Belize may have a certain nature to it that fits like a glove with the living vessels there. The one in Switzerland will probably be very different. We pass on to you these general guidelines, but the watch is living and individual. The Holy Spirit works with the individual persons involved.

In that way God fulfills His whole purpose in the big picture of the watch. Each watch becomes a thread in the great tapestry God is weaving. Each prayer is added to the golden bowls of incense, which are offered on the golden altar before the throne of God (Rev. 8:3–5).

The Lord is the Captain of every watch. Always, we take our direction from Him. We encourage you not to stick with a form all the time, because the Lord will come and the stream will change; so flow with the Lord. But we do suggest that you always love the Lord first—start with praise and worship. "Enter into His gates with thanksgiving, and into His courts with praise" (Ps. 100:4). That's how we are to approach Him.

The useful tips outlined in this chapter will help you facilitate the move of the Holy Spirit during your own Watch of the Lord.

1. Designate a watch leader.

The Holy Spirit always honors the appropriate order as established by church leadership. We have learned to designate a watch leader—someone whose task it is to be in charge. This leader is called the watch captain, and choosing the right person is essential for the long-term success of the watch. This is a position of God-given authority, being selected to lead intercession in the army of God. Even if yours is a small group, please allow yourself to be directed by the Lord when choosing a specific leader who will be responsible for protecting the anointing through loving leadership throughout the Watch of the Lord.

The captain you select may not necessarily be a "born leader," but instead someone who knows what it means to be continually "soaking" in the anointed presence of the Holy Spirit. This person should be a man or woman of prayer, someone who understands what it means to get into the presence of God on a regular basis and who can lead others there too via the anointing of intercessory prayer.

If your watch is in a local church, you may wish to designate as watch captain the senior pastor or an anointed servant selected by the pastor to perform this function. The captain must be one who is trained to listen to the voice of the Holy Spirit and keep the flow of the Watch of the Lord in the same vein. The watch captain must deter any attempts to divert attention away from the flow of the Holy Spirit, whether intentional or unintentional.

Alternate leaders should be chosen to fill in during times when the captain must be absent. This will guard against potential burnout. Although the watch captain may choose to share fresh prophetic scripture and thoughts pertinent to the watch, his or her primary function is to direct the watch—not necessarily preach or teach. Teaching or preaching should be kept to a minimum since the watch is set apart as a time to be with God and pray.

2. Appoint a watch communications officer.

The Bible was written down mainly by scribes—those who heard what God was saying to His people via the Holy Spirit and who diligently wrote it down. So we suggest that you also faithfully record the prophetic revelation poured out to you each week from heaven by appointing a watch communications officer, who is responsible for seeing there is a written record of the events and revelations that occur as you and your group gather to pray. The communications officer may also serve as an actual scribe—the person doing the writing.

It is a good idea to appoint one watch communications officer as well as three alternate scribes. The communications officer oversees the scribes and is ultimately responsible for the logs. For larger watches, the communications officer might have two or three alternates to take over during different parts of the watch, one at a time.

Commission each to record only the most pertinent events—the highlights—of the Watch of the Lord.

Ezekiel, Isaiah and Habakkuk were all such watchmen—scribes. Hearing from God and then writing down what He speaks is displayed throughout Scripture. The prophet Habakkuk wrote, "I will stand my watch and set myself on the rampart, and watch to see what He will say to me. . . . Then the LORD answered me and said: 'Write the vision and make it plain on tablets, that he may run who reads it'" (Hab. 2:1–2).

Ezekiel wrote, "I have made you a watchman for the house of Israel; therefore you shall hear a word from My mouth and warn them for Me" (Ezek. 33:7). Later still, the apostle Paul wrote, "Do not despise prophecies. Test all things; hold fast what is good" (1 Thess. 5:20–21).

When appropriate, during the watch share from the watch log of the previous week to show the pattern of prayer the Lord was directing then. After the scribe records the events of the watch, we request that he or she communicate to our office the most pertinent things expressed by the Holy Spirit so we can keep these revelations on file. We read each watch log in order to acquire the collective feeling of what the Holy Spirit is saying.

We also communicate with other watch groups to compare what the Holy Spirit is saying to the body of Christ via the many watch groups that are now located virtually around the globe—with more being added weekly! Through this networking we are able to strengthen and encourage one another as we confirm the word of the Lord to His church.

Here are some important things your watch communications officer, or scribe, should always remember:

- Come prepared with a notebook or laptop computer designated as a watch journal and something with which to write; inside it keep an accurate account of the events of each Watch of the Lord. A small tape recorder may also be helpful to record words from God or prophecies.

- Record all pertinent scripture verses shared, any new prophecies given, urgent prayer requests, prophetic songs, testimonies directly related to prayers answered from a previous watch and any prophetic prayers.

- If the scribe must be absent, the communications officer should assign an alternate scribe or arrange to have the service taped and notes taken afterward.

- We encourage those who are starting corporate watches to drop us a line or contact us by e-mail or fax so that we may pray for you. Give us your name, the watch captain's name, your church, your city and your country. If the Lord gives you a prophetic impression or you have a special testimony that you want to share about the watch, please drop us a line. We would appreciate hearing what the Holy Spirit is saying to the watch groups He is raising up around the globe.

3. Establish a Watch of the Lord protocol.

The watch captain can prevent most distractions by setting standards, or protocol to be observed during each and every watch. These should be recapped early in the evening each week so that newcomers will know what to expect. For instance:

- Children are welcome to participate in the watch. They can sing, dance, join in praise and worship, sleep or play quietly. The strength of the watch from the beginning has been that everyone can experience it, even people who have small children or babies. If families participating in the watch bring children and babies, the parents must be responsible for their children's behavior during the watch hours. It may work for your group to have the older children watch after the younger ones. Some welcome ways for them to pass the time might be quiet games or coloring books. Children should be instructed not to move around, run through the building or play in a loud and boisterous manner. We must, as a group, learn to keep

155

our focus always on the Lord. Children should never be outside the room where the watch is being held unless supervised by a parent. This is for their safety.

- Water, coffee and creamer are available throughout the night, but snacks are not suggested since the watch is set aside as a time of prayer and fasting. (See Joel 1:13–14.)

- The watch hours should be regular and established. Friday night seems to be the time that the Lord has anointed for us as the Watch of the Lord. This is also a practical time, since many people do not have to work on Saturdays and can take time that day to catch up on their sleep and recuperate from the rigors of all-night prayer. Those who attend should feel free to come and go quietly as necessary, but there should be no loitering outside the building or around the coffee pot. When necessary, appoint ushers to supervise the building.

- Those who become tired may feel free to "snooze in the anointing."

- Those who receive prophetic words, visions and scripture verses should write these down throughout the night and give them to the scribe or watch captain. Later in the night the watch captain may share some of these prophetic words and revelations, although this should be kept to a limit so as not to sidetrack the group. The watch captain should also screen prophetic words before reading them out loud.

- Although our primary focus is to minister to the Lord, a designated ministry team should be available to pray for people. The laying on of hands will be done by those appointed by the watch captain. Those who have a personal prophetic word for someone are requested to hold it until ministry time, and then wait for an OK from the watch captain before giving it.

- At some point during the evening, taking corporate communion is suggested. Bonnie and I believe in the power of sharing the body and the blood of the Lord's table in order to cleanse, build and unify. Intercession will usually flow much more powerfully during the last hours, once we have shared communion together.

4. Designate worship leaders.

Worship should be a major ingredient of your successful "watch recipe." If at all possible, Bonnie and I suggest that you designate more than one worship leader—or perhaps a worship leader and an alternate who can play guitar or piano as well as lead others in singing. One or more alternate leaders may help to take the pressure off the worship leader, but the hand-off should take place at a time that will not interrupt noticeably the flow of worship. Singers and other instrumentalists may be added as the Lord brings anointed worshipers into your midst.

Those who do not have a worship leader in their midst who is also an instrumentalist may wish to use praise and worship tapes. The song choices should include lively praise songs at first that build faith, then songs that lead to intimate worship. Afterward, you may want to step up the tempo again with more lively songs. Remember—the worship leader should help the congregation build their spiritual muscles.

You may also wish to purchase simple percussion instruments, such as maracas, tambourines, triangles, wooden sticks and bongos so the watchmen can participate.

Do not discount the importance of the prophetic dance. You may wish to designate an open area for the purpose of such dancing. The Lord often anoints His worshipers to dance before Him as David danced. As the Spirit moves in your midst, you may even see the anointing to dance prophetically come upon the children.

5. Intercession in the Watch of the Lord

Bonnie and I have noted that it is usually not until the later hours

157

of the watch that the spirit of intercession will fall. It seems to be only after we have spent considerable time before the Lord, loving Him in worship, that prayer reaches its maximum intensity. However, the spirit of prayer may fall suddenly during worship or even at the beginning of the watch.

While we want to stay sensitive to the move of the Holy Spirit and avoid trying to come up with our various "formulas," Bonnie and I have identified the following areas of intercession that we attempt to cover at every watch:

- Pray for the church of Jesus Christ locally, nationally and around the world. Maps of your city, state, nation and nations of the world—Israel in particular—are helpful in making points of contact during such intercession.

- Pray for all the world's watchmen and intercessors, asking the Lord to raise up more workers in His global harvest field.

- Pray for local government leaders, the governor of your state, the members of Congress and the Supreme Court, as well as the president. "I exhort you first of all that supplications, prayers, intercessions, and giving of thanks be made for all men, for kings and all who are in authority, that we may lead a quiet and peaceable life in all godliness and reverence" (1 Tim. 2:1–2).

- Pray for the peace of Jerusalem.

- Pray for national concerns, international tranquility and economic stability to facilitate the End-Time harvest.

- Pray specifically for ministry leaders and area pastors with whom there is a commitment for consistent intercession.

- Pray for the households and children of the watchmen, both present and absent. In our watch, every young person is prayed over each time we meet, prayed for by name and covered. The teenagers love that anointing. They come as a whole group and get in line to be prayed for all the time.

• Pray for the elderly, the lonely, the forgotten and those in prison.

• Pray for the requests of individuals that have been submitted to the group during the week. These requests should be kept brief in nature and can even be offered up collectively before the Lord, unless the watch captain is impressed to pray at length and more specifically over a certain need. Prayer for these requests is usually best in the last hour of the watch.

• Ask the captain of the watch or the designated ministry team to pray for and minister any prophetic words to those individuals who desire personal prayer during the watch.

We have seen awesome results to prayer during these all-night watch meetings. We have learned always to be ready to make fresh prophetic intercession according to the Holy Spirit's instruction from watch to watch.

6. Corporate communion and giving

There is great blessing in sharing the Lord's Table with those present at each Watch of the Lord. As Bonnie and I mentioned earlier, often we have received fresh impartation and an increase of the anointing as we have taken communion in the course of the watch. At times the Lord's presence has manifested in our midst, bringing outbursts of joyous laughter.

In addition to serving communion at our watches in Charlotte, we also take up an offering for the poor and homeless in our area. As the Lord increases your blessings and adds to the number of people who pray and watch with you weekly, we sincerely hope that you will find a project in your area to support, such as the poor or those in prison. The support of the underprivileged is an ongoing need in our midst, and ministering to those less fortunate will bring a reward as well as bring honor to the Lord.

Remember, then, that the Watch of the Lord can be held by anyone who carries a burden to pray. A church may start such a group, or even a single individual. All it takes is a commitment and a heart to pray.

We are praying for you as you begin your Watch of the Lord. You are a vital part of God's army. If you are starting a corporate watch, contact us with your e-mail address or your regular address so we can keep in touch with you. We pray for all the watch captains in the world. When we hold conferences, we always hold a watch. Perhaps you can come for training and experience a corporate watch.

Remember, when God's people pray, awesome things happen.

Blessed is he who watches.

—Revelation 16:15

11

The Individual Watch

---

§

BONNIE AND I believe that God's word for this hour is to pray corporately. God is calling us to corporate prayer during this hour. The entire church is called to pray, and anyone can be a watchman. If you have a burden for the people of the world, regardless of their race, background or circumstances, you are called to watch and pray!

Remember, just one watchman could have prevented the *Titanic* disaster if he had been properly equipped. "The effective, fervent prayer of a righteous man avails much" (James 5:16). The Bible also says a single person who prays can put a thousand to flight: "One man of you shall chase a thousand: for the LORD your God, he it is that fighteth for you, as he hath promised you" (Josh. 23:10, KJV). A single watchman for a house can save a whole family, a whole city, even a whole nation.

I have set watchmen on your walls, O Jerusalem; they shall

never hold their peace day or night. You who make mention of the LORD, do not keep silent, and give Him no rest till He establishes and till He makes Jerusalem a praise in the earth.

—ISAIAH 62:6-7

Your Jerusalem can be your household, and God wants to make it a praise on the earth.

If you want to find out if any watches are being held in your area, contact our office. If your pastor gets the vision for a watch—great! Have a watch in your church. But if your pastor doesn't want to do this, you can watch in your home. Call two or three fanatics who love Jesus as you do and say, "Come over. We are going to pray." If you can't find anyone, you can do it as I did at the Western Wall, where I watched all night by myself.

MY PERSONAL WATCHES

EVERY YEAR FOR the last fifteen years I have held miracle services in Jerusalem during the Feast of Tabernacles. The healing power of Christ has touched and transformed many Jews and Gentiles. Some of these services have been held in the largest convention center in Jerusalem, called the *Binyanei Ha'Uma*. The glory of the Lord has been very apparent in many of these historic services.

One day some years ago while I was in Jerusalem, I heard the Lord speak to me saying that His presence would meet me at the Western Wall. After a glorious healing service, I quickly changed and made my way to the Wall by midnight. Suddenly the extraordinary love and glory of God surrounded me. All sense of time was swallowed up in His presence. I simply adored and worshiped the Lord God of Israel for hours.

As the first rays of golden light streaked across the deep Jerusalem skies, I put notes of prayer requests into the crevices of this ancient Wall. *Where had the hours gone?* I wondered. I grasped then how a thousand years in His presence will be like a day.

This was my first experience of watching and praying alone at the

164

Western Wall. I have repeated this experience many times. It is difficult to explain in words the utter delight of watching alone in His presence.

There are occasions and circumstances that will require you to watch alone. I pray that the same grace and glory that I experienced at the Wall will surround you. Know that there is no reason to feel discouraged because you are praying alone or as a married couple. The key that will unlock the secret of watching is the joy of His presence. The Scriptures say, "In Your presence is fullness of joy!" (Ps. 16:11).

INDIVIDUAL WATCH GUIDELINES

Be led by the Holy Spirit.

As you answer this call to watch and pray over your family, let yourself be led by the Holy Spirit. As you welcome the Holy Spirit, He brings the lordship of Jesus in all areas of your life. He will flow as a gracious, healing river throughout your time to watch and pray.

> For as many as are led by the Spirit of God, these are sons of God. . . . Likewise the Spirit also helps in our weaknesses. For we do not know what we should pray for as we ought, but the Spirit Himself makes intercession for us with groanings which cannot be uttered. Now He who searches the hearts knows what the mind of the Spirit is, because He makes intercession for the saints according to the will of God.
>
> —ROMANS 8:14, 26–27

The Holy Spirit is the Helper. Let Him help. You will find that watching will not be a labor, but a joy and refreshing.

Select a specific time and place.

Choose a specific time when you can watch regularly. One suggestion is every Friday night from 7 P.M. till midnight. You don't have to feel any great emotion about the time. As far as watch times go, do what is practical. Whatever the time frame you set for your individual watch, we believe God is emphasizing what He told Gideon: "Go in the strength you have and save Israel out of Midian's hand. Am I not sending you?" (Judg. 6:14, NIV). The important thing is to take your place as a watchman whether you feel like it or not.

Set aside a specific place where you can watch in your house. Jesus instructed us to go into our "closet" to pray. Daniel had a chamber set aside for this; Habakkuk had a watchtower. Find your place.

Start with praise and worship.

The key to a successful watch—individual or corporate—is the presence of the Lord. When I praise the Lord, I establish a throne from which the King of kings can establish His lordship over my life and all my concerns. "But You are holy, enthroned in the praises of Israel" (Ps. 22:3).

God's habitation is the realm of the praises of His people. If you want to spend quality time in His presence, approach Him in an appropriate and scriptural manner, giving Him adoration and honor as the Lord God, King of the universe. "Enter into His gates with thanksgiving, and into His courts with praise. Be thankful to Him, and bless His name" (Ps. 100:4). "Therefore by Him let us continually offer the sacrifice of praise to God, that is, the fruit of our lips, giving thanks to His name" (Heb. 13:15). Praise is the river of love and adoration flowing from our hearts into the presence of the King of kings.

I often encourage people to "step into the vision" as they watch. The Holy Spirit gives us awesome glimpses of heaven in Scripture. Just chew on these scriptures; meditate on them, appreciating and loving the truth that God is giving you about Himself, His presence, His glory and heaven. Release your heart to join what's going on and what the Scripture describes. Join the cry of the creatures who are saying, "Holy, holy, holy." Worship the Lord with those words for a while.

Let your heart ride on the wind of the Holy Spirit in total abandonment, trusting in the Holy Spirit. Then you'll sense a communing with the greatness of the Lord. Your spirit will start becoming one with the truth of that scripture. You will become intimate with the Word itself.

Several times the Lord has allowed me to get into a river of adoration by stepping into these heavenly visions recounted in scriptures, such as this one in Isaiah:

> In the year that King Uzziah died, I saw the Lord sitting on a throne, high and lifted up, and the train of His robe filled the temple. Above it stood seraphim; each one had six wings: with two he covered his face, with two he covered his feet, and with two he flew. And one cried to another and said: "Holy, holy, holy is the LORD of hosts; the whole earth is full of His glory!"
>
> And the posts of the door were shaken by the voice of him who cried out, and the house was filled with smoke.
>
> So I said: "Woe is me, for I am undone! Because I am a man of unclean lips, and I dwell in the midst of a people of unclean lips; for my eyes have seen the King, the LORD of hosts."
>
> —ISAIAH 6:1–5

Other "vision" scriptures that may help you are Ezekiel 1 and Revelation 4 and 5 (in their entirety).

For a successful watch, the requirement is intimacy. Let your heart be possessed by love of the divine Bridegroom, Jesus. Lose yourself in His holiness, greatness and goodness. Responding to His holiness will lead you deeper into worship. Responding to His multifaceted greatness will lead you into praise. Responding to His goodness toward you will move you into heartfelt thanksgiving.

Sometimes, music from anointed CDs and tapes will assist you in getting into this river of adoration and worship. Worship helps seat us in heavenly places. The watchman's premier perspective must be through the eyes of the Lord, who has already overcome. Seeing through His eyes affects our perspective of everything that happens in this realm. Focus on the Lord, not on adverse circumstances or the things of the earth.

These sessions of worship could go for hours. There have been seasons in our corporate watch where our worship has gone on for five hours, and it seemed like ten minutes. Or it could last for an hour. Flow with the river of God's Spirit. The Holy Spirit is the Lord of the watch.

In our corporate watch we will dance before the Lord in the anointing. I have done this also when I am watching alone. "Let them praise His name with the dance; let them sing praises to Him with the timbrel and harp" (Ps. 149:3).

Worshiping by singing in the Spirit is also a great help, especially when making a transition from worship to intercession.

Giving a priority to worship and praise not only gives you entrance to the presence of the King, but it also helps you bind back satanic powers from your situation. More praising will result in less necessity of laboring in heavy warfare prayer.

Keep a watch log.

Keeping a watch log or journal helps the whole process in the watch. Write down impressions, words and visions the Lord gives you in these seasons of praise and worship.

As you watch, the Commander in Chief of the watch will speak to your heart on occasion. He will give a vision, a prophetic word of encouragement, a word of knowledge or a scripture. Note it on your watch log. It will help you see how God has used you when you hear the results of answered watch prayer. It helps you learn how the Holy Spirit moves. By looking back, you can see His traits and personality revealed through the streams of revelation.

Keeping a journal or log also disciples you in receiving and interpreting revelation. As you are faithful, the Lord will give you more. With a log you can see the times you heard and saw clearly and the times when you missed the mark—misinterpreted something or only got it partly correct.

Follow a scriptural pattern.

You may want to pattern your watch after scriptures by creating a prayer track for the whole watch. Sometimes I will follow a prayer track for my thoughts according to Psalm 23. I break it down into various ways of exalting the Lord: as my shepherd (*Jehovah Rohi*), as my provider (*Jehovah Jireh*), as my healer (*Jehovah Rophe*), as my sanctifier (*Jehovah McKaddishem*), as my peace (*Jehovah Shalom*), as my righteousness (*Jehovah Tsidkenu*), as my banner of victory (*Jehovah Nissi*) and as the ever-present Lord (*Jehovah Shammah*).

"So this day," I tell myself, "I shall not want for guidance, provision, healing, sanctification, peace, righteousness, victory or His presence." Then I break the psalm into various portions and pray extemporaneously as the Spirit leads.

The Lord's Prayer is another wonderful pattern for prayer.

Put on the armor of God.

After you have established a sense of communion with the Lord through your praise and worship, you may want to go into prayer warfare. Put on the full armor of God:

> Therefore take up the whole armor of God, that you may be able to withstand in the evil day, and having done all, to stand.
>
> Stand therefore, having girded your waist with truth, having put on the breastplate of righteousness, and having shod your feet with the preparation of the gospel of peace; above all, taking the shield of faith with which you will be able to quench all the fiery darts of the wicked one. And take the helmet of salvation, and the sword of the Spirit, which is the word of God; praying always with all prayer and supplication in the Spirit, being watchful to this end with all perseverance and supplication for all the saints.
>
> —EPHESIANS 6:13–18

Any general will tell you that high morale in troops determines victory or defeat. It is important, whatever your circumstance, that you approach the Lord with faith and not a sense of discouragement and defeat. (Anointed music helps do this.) He is a miracle-working God who responds to faith.

Pray for your household.

Sometime during the watch, I encourage people to pray aggressively for members of their household. Watching releases deliverance and household salvation. Remember Paul and Silas? As they watched and prayed, the entire prison foundation was shaken. The shackles broke and fell off everyone. Everyone's chains were loosed, including the spiritual chains of the family of the guard. Paul and Silas were the watchmen for the whole prison.

If you watch and commune with the Lord, shackles over your family will break and fall; prison doors will open. As you pray for your spouse and your children, confess Scripture over them (make sure you mention your family members by name).

Pray your list.

After praying for your immediate family, you may have a prayer list of those who need your prayers. We use note cards with the names of people, people groups and ministries for which we regularly intercede. These serve as points of contact for our faith and prayers. Plus, they keep us from having to remember everything! By 4 A.M., you can be a little fuzzy!

Pray for your pastor and others serving the Lord, such as missionaries and evangelists. Pray for Israel. Pray for your local church needs, your neighborhood, your local schools, your city and your nation. Then take some time to pray for nations and for the lost to be saved.

Pray in the Spirit.

Praying in the Spirit for two or three hours a week during your watch won't hurt you, and you never know what you may be praying through! When you pray in tongues, you will be "building yourselves up on your most holy faith" (Jude 20).

Take communion.

As you watch and pray, it is essential that you realize you are coming to the Lord on the foundation of the finished work of Christ on Calvary. Jesus Christ—crucified, dead, buried and resurrected on the third day—is the basis on which all our prayers are received and answered by our heavenly Father. In the final analysis, how you feel when you watch and pray does not matter. It is Jesus, Jesus, Jesus! His work on the cross is eternally excellent and all sufficient for every need, across all the galaxies of the universe.

To help us focus on this truth, we always take communion in our corporate watch. When possible I recommend the same practice when you watch individually. Take some bread and grape juice, pray over it and partake of the Lord's supper. Go through a season of repentance when the Holy Spirit leads. Then release forgiveness to those whom you need to forgive.

The Captain of Hosts will come down as you partake of the elements to sanctify, cleanse and refresh you; He will give you a new start. On the basis of Jesus' shed blood, the power of the curse is broken, chains of oppression fall away from your family and the blessings of God are released.

Truimph in Christ.

End the watch on a triumphant note. Exalt the Lord and declare Him Lord and victor over every area of your life. "But thanks be to God, who always leads us in His triumph in Christ, and manifests through us the sweet aroma of the knowledge of Him in every place" (2 Cor. 2:14, NAS).

Just do it.

As you take up the call, you will find that it will start transforming you. You will start hearing the Lord's voice more accurately since you are spending more time with Him. There will be a new authority in you to witness and to overcome words of darkness since you are taking your place consistently in God's army as a watchman intercessor. You will start seeing prophetically, and you will receive words of knowledge with greater ease. And you will see answers to prayer, like the importunate widow who would not give up (Luke 18:5).

Finally, make sure that you are consistent in keeping the watch. You may watch daily or a few hours per week on a specific day. Whatever you do, please don't hesitate to take up this call to become a watchman for your family, church and nation. Don't discuss it or study it or analyze it. Just do it.

A watchman from Idaho who watches by herself told us about one private watch in January 1998 when she had a worship tape on:

> When the tape finished, I heard music and singing. It was the most beautiful music I had ever heard, and I kept listening for about ten minutes. The words were sung in the Spirit. Then I didn't hear any more.
>
> Then in February, at least once every day I would hear the music from heaven, sometimes singing, sometimes instruments. I had opened the ears of my spirit to be aware of the music. Then in March, I began to hear the heavenly music all the time.

She says that when she contacted our office, she was told that I had prayed in March, asking the Lord to open heaven for the watchmen. She continued:

> I saw that God had answered his prayer for me through the gift He has given me to hear actual singing of the ministering angels, singing in glorious praise to Jesus. By His mercy, He has opened to me the windows of heaven every moment of the day and night, and I am eternally grateful.

Did you notice what this watchman said: "I had opened the ears of my spirit...."? Watching will change you, just as I promised.

Remember the ad of a shoe company and apply it regarding watching and praying. I give you a word from the Lord: *Just do it!*

Even if you are involved in a corporate watch, you still need to be alert in the anointing over your household. When you are alert to listen to the Lord about your children, God will speak to you about their needs. Watching is praying, but it is not just getting down on your knees. It's listening to the Lord and praying by the power of the Spirit. Let me tell you what I mean.

Our Daughter Anna

ON THE NIGHT of May 7, 1998, I was in my office when a heavy burden of intercession came over me. I felt as if there were a weight on my heart that I could not explain, that if I didn't get down on my knees, I would burst. All I could do was get on my face before the Lord in strong intercession. I cried out to the Lord. I prayed in tongues. I didn't know what I was praying for, but I knew I was praying through to victory for something very important. After about three hours, it lifted. The Lord did not tell me what was going to happen.

That night our daughter Anna was up late studying for final exams for college. Before I went to bed, I felt impressed to tell her not to drive my car to school the next day. "Take your mother's Jeep," I insisted. There was no reason I knew of to make these arrangements. Anna always drove my car to school in the mornings. After repeating this two or three times, I made her promise. She rolled her eyes at me and said, "OK, Dad, I promise."

In a few hours she was on the road in the early morning rain. That day Anna took a route she was not accustomed to. With the morning sun in her eyes, she came upon a hairpin curve and lost control of the car. The Jeep skidded off the road at about 35 mph and ran head-on into a tree. The car was totaled, and Anna was pinned inside.

When Bonnie and I arrived a few minutes later, the emergency rescue team was just extracting Anna from the Jeep. Her body was in braces and she was strapped to a stretcher. Policemen and fire and emergency personnel were everywhere. One of the men told Bonnie, "I've worked nearly thirty calls like this. This is the first time the person in the vehicle was still alive." The firemen, the policemen and the rescue personnel all told us again and again that accidents like this always resulted in massive injuries and usually death. They surveyed the scene, shook their heads and said again and again, "It's a miracle your daughter is alive."

After the ambulance left for the hospital, the policeman present pointed again to the demolished Jeep. "Those airbags saved her life," he commented. We knew that God and His angels had also been on assignment. I also knew then why I had been so burdened in prayer just hours before. I remembered that my car had no airbags. If Anna had driven my car instead of her mother's, the outcome of the accident would have been altogether different.

Anna suffered bad breaks in both her legs. She is now fully recovered; doctors expect her to have no long-term ill effects.

One watchman can save an entire house if the watchman is alert. The thief who comes to steal, kill and destroy passes by the house whose watch lamps are burning brightly as we stay alert in the anointing.

I feel that the enemy had a plan to kill one of my children, and the Lord saved her brilliantly. The Lord sets a table for us in the midst of our enemies (Ps. 23:5). He gives us the victory, but not through our own might or our own sword. We have times of warfare, but the Lord is the One who delivers us.

The morning of the crash, a watch captain from the Atlanta area called our office. That morning as she arose, she felt as if God connected her to our family. She started seeing pictures of our children, and she started praying for them. She felt such an intercessory burden for our children that she took off early from work to pray for them. She called our office and then faxed what she had been receiving in prayer. Here is part of it:

> "There's been an attempt by the enemy to choke out life, but I cut this away from you with My sword of truth," says the Lord. "The tentacles that would ring around and strangle, I rip away from you now. I will not allow the foxes to spoil My vineyard. Your seed has been fertile and true. I pour My blood out on your battlefield to be a barrier against the enemy. The devastation and evil that had been plotted has been turned away."

So we see the interlinking of the body of Christ. And we see clearly the need, the responsibility and the joy of being alert in the anointing and of being watchful in your own family. A year later,

Anna's doctor said she was doing remarkably well. He was surprised that she was walking and jogging and wearing sandals and high heels. He does not expect any future problems or complications.

Our victories lie in our secret lives with Christ.

START WHERE YOU ARE

YES, IT'S TRUE that God's heart is for our nation and her cities, as well as for all nations. He wants to use His people to bring healing and restoration. And yes, it's true that I have a healing ministry. But it's also true that I did not start my ministry by praying for the sick and seeing them healed, delivered and raised from the dead. No, I started at the level where I was and began to use what faith I had right then. As I released that faith in praying for the sick, I moved from faith to faith, progressing by levels from one to the next until I began doing the works of Christ.

That same principle works in the lives of all Christians, regardless of the size or scope of the work. Start where you are, use what you have and God will bring the increase once you are found faithful.

If nobody else is watching in your family, take it up. Don't put that responsibility on someone else; it is yours. Welcome it. Don't put it on your husband or your wife. First, do it yourself. Start with the strength you have. Don't feel guilty if you fall asleep. Your body will get addicted to prayer, and your body clock will adjust. Then, as you have a living experience with the Bridegroom, out of your own enthusiasm and your own spirit, share it with others. God is issuing an invitation for all those with a heart for ministry and intercession to come and be watchmen. He will meet you there, bless your efforts and cause the increase.

§

Where two or three
are gathered together in My name,
I am there in the midst of them.

———————

—MATTHEW 18:20

12

God Plus One Is a Majority

§

THE WATCH OF the Lord is a ministry that is simple to begin, yet full of purpose and destiny. Anyone can start a Watch of the Lord. It may begin under the auspices of a church or ministry, or it may begin in someone's home. It may be attended by fifty or a hundred people, or it may start out small—and even remain so. It may even begin with one individual. Yet the results for God's kingdom will be very large indeed.

In fact, the watch is for every individual, at least one per family. Every mother and father can become a watchman. Every grandmother and grandfather can be a watchman. Everyone who has ever wanted to go to the mission field can be a watchman. Every family needs a watchman to take his or her place on the wall of intercession for his or her household.

Bonnie and I have seen countless miracles in our watch services on Friday nights—regardless of the numbers present. What matters is prayer—the fervent prayers of the watchman!

All the Holy Spirit needs is a warm body with the willingness to be used by Him to stand in the gap. Even if your watch is only once a month, start somewhere. Once you begin, be committed to carry on to the best of your abilities.

THE DAY OF SMALL BEGINNINGS

HISTORY TESTIFIES THAT small prayer groups can be a mighty force in spearheading global revival. God's work of restoration always began with a remnant. One man, Abraham, stood in the gap for Lot and his family and saved them from destruction. One man, Moses, saved the Israelites from God's wrath over and over. One woman, Esther, was in the right place at the right time to intercede on behalf of her people, the Jews.

Gideon and three hundred men handpicked by God routed the Midianites. In the upper room just one hundred twenty followers of Christ received the Holy Spirit and began the church. Even in our day, the remnant of the Jews that survived the Holocaust birthed the nation of Israel. Small groups—even "groups" of one plus God—can change the world.

The strategic importance and power of trained and faithful believers who will watch in prayer for their families, cities, churches and nations is illustrated by the following:

> The gratitude of every home in our Island, in our Empire, and indeed throughout the world goes out to the British airmen who, undaunted by odds, unwearied in their constant challenge and mortal danger, are turning the tide of the World War by their prowess and by their devotion. Never in the field of human conflict was so much owed by so many to so few. All hearts go out to the fighter pilots, whose brilliant actions we see with our own eyes day after day; but we must never forget that all the time, night after night, month after month, our bomber squadrons travel far into [enemy territory], find their targets in the darkness by the highest navigational skill, aim their attacks,

often under the heaviest fire, often with serious loss, with the deliberate careful discrimination, and inflict shattering blows upon the whole of the technical and war-making structure of the [enemy's] power.[1]

In Scripture, we are warned not to despise the day of small beginnings. Contained within that concept is the entire mystery of seedtime and harvest. Who would ever believe that contained within the blueprint of one small, seemingly inconsequential seed would be the potential of a mighty, spreading oak? But that is the mysterious way of the kingdom—taking what is weak and small and glorifying it, and from it making a great nation. Look at Abraham, who began the nation of Israel by fathering a son in his old age when it appeared he was already too old.

Again, we see the people of the nation Israel—small, seemingly inconsequential, yet laden with destiny due to their highly favored status as God's chosen people.

So the Watch of the Lord can begin small. You never know—the Lord may cause it to grow into a very large group. Or it may remain small. Don't expect God necessarily to enlarge your numbers. The Lord can do much with little, and a handful of people praying together powerfully in agreement can accomplish great things in the kingdom.

During World War II Germany possessed the elements to ultimately develop nuclear weapons. Allied forces were racing against time in an effort to prevent Hitler from attaining this final advantage for world domination. In February 1943, in the thick of harsh winter, six Norwegian saboteurs finally managed to infiltrate the German heavy water factory at Vemork, Norway, halting production. This successful raid forced Berlin to attempt to move the plant and its inventory. In a second successful feat of espionage, British intelligence positioned a single saboteur aboard the ferry carrying Germany's heavy water supply. The agent sank the ferry, and with it sank Germany's hopes of getting an atomic bomb before the end of World War II. This was the first nuclear counterproliferation operation in history.[2]

THE POWER OF THE FEW

THERE IS PRIVILEGE, anointing, grace and victory that come with the agreement of two or more. "Where two or three are gathered together in My name, I am there in the midst of them" (Matt. 18:20). If two or three or more are praying in agreement, awesome things start happening.

The history of Gideon's army given to us in Judges 7 is precious because it is proof that God can move in great power with a few committed believers. Gideon took a huge army out to do battle against their enemy, the Midianites. Through a series of encounters with the Lord that took place along the way to the battle, Gideon was instructed to cut back the numbers of his army again and yet again, so that in the end only three hundred men and their horses remained. But these three hundred were the fiercest, most courageous, vigilant and persevering of all Gideon's warriors.

Greatly outnumbered by the enemy, Gideon and his men set their hands to the battle, and the Lord empowered them with His strength, grace and heavenly strategies. Their weapons were unusual indeed. Each man had a trumpet in one hand and a pitcher with a torch in it in the other hand. How could such a strange-looking army ever hope to succeed against the enemy, who outnumbered them several times over? How could such foolish weapons ever prevail against a formidable foe?

God's power was released from heaven when Gideon and his men obeyed Him and used their "mighty" weapons against the enemy. Gideon's small army would have been the laughingstock of the Midianites had they seen them coming. But they didn't. In those days, battles traditionally stopped at sundown since no one could see the enemy or navigate the terrain in the dark. This time, however, God told Gideon to strike at night.

At the beginning of the middle watch, which lasted from the hours of 10 P.M. until 2 A.M., Gideon's army readied their strike. Gideon's three hundred men flanking the Midianite encampment were shrouded in the darkness, their torches unseen inside the clay pitchers. Three hundred trumpets hung silent, waiting for the signal from the captain, Gideon.

The Lord had given Gideon the perfect strategy: surprise! The enemy was expecting a huge army to come in daylight—trumpets blaring and banners waving. Instead, the attack came at night from a small band of elite warriors.

At the right moment, Gideon blew his trumpet. Then his men, who were surrounding the camp of the enemy, broke their pitchers (revealing three hundred blazing torches), blew their trumpets and shouted. And they just stood there. The enemy army, swarming in the dark, panicked, turned on itself and devoured one another. Those who survived fled. So perfect was the strategy and timing of God's plan that Gideon's men did not have to lift a sword.

The victory that day went to Gideon and his small army, showing us that large numbers are not necessary for a victorious outcome when the Lord is involved. A few elite warriors with the desire to use the Lord's weapons to usher in the Lord's deliverance can utterly defeat the enemy and bring in total triumph.

THE STRATEGIES OF HEAVEN

As GIDEON'S THREE hundred men marched out in the power of the Spirit, God gave them His strategies for routing the enemy:

1. Go out at night.

2. Lay in wait.

3. At the given word, rise in union with great shouting, with the blast of the shofar and with lights lifted up in the darkness.

4. Do not turn back until the enemy is utterly destroyed and the land of the inheritance is repossessed.

This fourfold strategy is our experience in the watch. We go out at night when the enemy most often works to destroy and oppress, using spiritual weapons and divine strategies that change from week to week under God's command.

The shofar was also used to awaken those who might have fallen asleep at their posts. God's trumpet call to His church today challenges us to awaken and take our rightful positions along the walls of prayer. After we blow the shofar, we shout to the Lord as Gideon's men did, giving a victory cheer. We sing praise to our God, letting demonic forces hear the dreaded name of Jesus, their Conqueror. We dance before the Lord, trampling the works of the enemy under our feet in a prophetic action symbolic of final victory.

The Watch of the Lord is a worldwide assault on the forces of darkness, a surprise attack that no one was expecting! We let our lights shine in the darkness and see many answers to prayer! And we don't give up the watch. We keep coming back to stand in the breach on the walls.

God is in the process of forming an army of prayer soldiers who are trained to attack. In homes, churches and other gathering places across America and in other lands, Christians are sharpening their weapons, lighting their torches and standing alert for the Holy Spirit's directives. As He moves, they aim their concerted prayers at evil strongholds. Crime, abortion, violence, immorality, injustice, racism and anti-Semitism—all of these sources of spiritual oppression are being targeted. God's secret forces, marching to His cadence, battle through the night, claiming victory after victory in the realm of the Spirit.

Let me tell you about some of God's secret forces that have been gathering together for watches—in prisons!

THE WATCH IN PRISONS

SEVERAL YEARS AGO, the Holy Spirit spoke to us and said, "The prisons will be like monasteries." Monasteries are places of holiness and devotion to intercession. As the Watch of the Lord began to connect with prisoners, the Holy Spirit swept through with a move of intercession, deliverance and refreshing.

The Holy Spirit is reminding us that it is not the pious and religious who have hearts full of love for Him; it is those who have been forgiven the greatest offense (Luke 7:47). In that love for Him, God is transforming many prisoners into powerful intercessors with great authority. Their authority is born out of their humility before God and the simplicity of their faith.

From an Alabama watch group who holds watches in prisons, we hear that people are soaking in worship in the prison watches. "The tender presence of the Lord is filling these meetings, and many lost prisoners are being converted just in worship."

This group tells of one prisoner who was very cold and angry, scowling and huffing the entire time he was in a service. This man suffered from blood clots in his legs, and his feet were swollen. He had not worn shoes in months because of the swelling, and he was barely walking on crutches.

The Holy Spirit instructed some men to pray for him. They anticipated that the prisoner would react negatively; instead, he began to weep and weep. The Lord broke through his hardness, and he cried, laughed and praised God before falling out under the power of the Holy Spirit.

Two weeks later the watchman who had prayed with him hardly recognized him. He didn't use crutches, and he had shoes on. The Lord had truly made him a different man.

In the same prison another young man who was serving four life sentences came to a worship service. The Lord pointed out to the watchman that this prisoner was the scariest, meanest, toughest man he'd ever seen in prison. God wanted him to grasp the wonder of his coming transformation.

As this prisoner continued to attend the services, God melted his heart and showed him the Person and nature of Christ. He became more and more beautiful and more and more in love with Jesus.

We also received the report of an inmate who had worshiped Satan for seven years giving his heart to Christ after witnessing the power of the Holy Spirit at a four-hour prayer meeting in his prison. He testified that he had tried to enter the room where the prayer watch was being held, but he could not go in because a large man dressed in clothes of white (an angel) was guarding the door!

The following week, he went to the meeting and was immediately slain in the Spirit. He gave his heart to Christ and he spent the next four hours laughing and rolling on the floor under the Holy Spirit's power. He is now falling in love with Jesus and thankful for his new life.

LETTERS FROM PRISONERS

A PRISONER FROM Arkansas wrote us, saying:

> I have kept one full watch each month this year and several partial watches. I value your prayers at your watch for us in prison. On March 26 I felt the Lord's presence come upon me in the afternoon, and you were on my mind. That evening just before the intercessory prayer meeting here I received your monthly newsletter on "Developing a Healing and Deliverance Ministry." I hoped we would have that kind of ministry here one day.
>
> That very night a gentleman in the prayer meeting displayed a need for deliverance. On Saturday, eight of us prayed with this brother again, and the anointing came, and we cast out evil spirits in Jesus' name. In one hour it was all done, and the brother wept as he "came to," and we all wept and rejoiced together. Though we had little training, Jesus sure blessed us that day.

All of us take things for granted, as this prisoner's letter about a watch reminded us:

> God was here as some openly wept, laughed and were literally drunk in the Holy Spirit. There were words of exhortation, praise, words of wisdom, words of knowledge and a general oneness in Christ that many take for granted in well-established

churches on the outside. There is much opposition because of it. There are bondages of drugs, alcohol, homosexuality, hatred, violence and controlling spirits.

Please intercede with us for these areas. Surely God is raising up an army filled with His power and love behind prison walls.

The humility of the prisoners is humbling to me. One prisoner wrote us, "We received a prophetic word that we are called into the priesthood, like those of the order of Melchizedek. We are to serve others and make sacrifices for them with our very lives. We feel that this is done through intercessory prayer."

Another prisoner from Alabama wrote, "I truly believe God has called me to intercede for things I know nothing about. I'm burdened to pray every day, sometimes praying for hours in the Spirit. Prayer is real. I'm experiencing rivers of living waters. They never run dry."

Changed lives bring changed attitudes, as shown by this inmate's letter:

We have seen the church body grow here, and the fire of God has been released with refreshing. Great things are happening, and Jesus alone is being glorified.

The enemy is trying some strategies. The warden assigned me to work in the compost pits. They are six feet deep. The kitchen slop is mixed with paper, straw and animal refuse so it all can decay. The temperature here is extremely high, and a terrible steam of methane and ammonia gases rise from it, as well as all kinds of insects.

As I went into that first pit, I said, "Lord Jesus, I really hate to carry You with me into this terrible place, but wherever I go, You go." Immediately, His presence flooded my soul.

WATCH TESTIMONIES

YES, THE POWER of God is present in the watch to tear down the strongholds of the enemy—even cancer. A young man from South Carolina was brought to our watch. He had cancer that had spread to his liver and brain.

At the watch, he received prayer and ministry and fell out in the power of the Spirit. When he was lying on the floor, he kept hearing "It is finished. It is finished. It is finished."

He returned to his doctors three days later. They informed him that it was pointless to continue more radiation and chemotherapy because, after his brain surgery, his cancer count had climbed from thirty-one to forty-one (fifteen being normal). They were afraid that this particular cancer was immune to treatment.

Nevertheless, this man stood his ground. They ran another test, and when the report came back a few days later, the count was twelve! This man and his wife then requested a full body scan, and the results showed that everything was clear except for an area in the brain that was inconclusive. They believe it was scar tissue and swelling from the recent brain surgery. God used this opportunity to bring glory and honor to His name.

During a prophetic ministry conference in Charlotte in 1995, I was a guest speaker. I announced the watch on Friday night, then felt impressed by the Lord to say, "Some of you who commit to stay all night will find that when you get home, the Lord has answered prayers you've been praying for years for your family."

A couple from Texas decided to come to the watch. The husband says that his first reaction was, "There's no way I can stay up all night." But his wife, who felt that this was a word of knowledge for them, said, "We're staying."

The very night they were at the watch, the Lord caught up with their adult son, who had been running for years from the Lord. That same night, his wife left him and nis dog died! He cried out to the Lord and was radically saved and transformed. Since then, the Lord restored his marriage (and gave him a new dog).

This couple from Texas who kept their first watch with us in Charlotte are now watch captains at a Friday night watch in their own church. "We are now awake every Friday night from 10 P.M. to 6 A.M."

Their son tells of another time he was affected by someone else interceding for him during a watch. This time it was his wife. He had suffered with chronic back pain due to a childhood accident. After his marriage was restored, his wife was at a watch in Dallas. She received a word in which the Lord told her to tell her husband, "The season of affliction is over. If he will seek Me in the morning, he will no longer need pills." That's exactly what happened, and he was healed.

The watch is a time for intimacy with Jesus, for healing, warfare, prayer, praise, worship—and fun! During a watch in Charlotte in 1997, a teenager came up to the platform and showed the watch captain his hands. They were covered in gold dust. The teenager told Bonnie and I that as he lay on the floor, having been slain in the Spirit, he saw a vision of Jesus pouring out gold dust on several people. As he got up from the floor, he saw gold dust on his hands. A woman also showed us gold dust on her hands. Many people then began to notice gold dust on their hands, faces and clothes.

A woman from a watch held regularly in Georgia told us what she saw one watch night in 1998:

> I could see into a part of heaven. Lord Jesus and His angels were present. Then I saw gold glory dust being poured all over the people who had their hands raised up in worship. The glory dust was the purity of God's Spirit being poured out on all who would worship and receive Him. Suddenly the glory dust turned into the blood of Jesus. Since it is His Blood that cleanses us, all who were touched by the glory dust were cleansed and purified.
>
> Then I saw different churches from all over the world. The persecuted church of China received a tremendous amount of the glory dust . . . Many other foreign nations received much from the Lord. In the U.S. there were some churches that did receive the glory dust; however, in many only one or two flakes of glory dust would fall on one to three people in the congregation. These one to three saints would be grateful. . . .
>
> I also saw angels gather around churches and fan the glory dust as it fell with their wings.

Isn't life with Jesus great fun?

THE WATCH OF THE LORD AROUND THE WORLD

HAVE YOU DECIDED to become a part of what the Lord is doing around the world in this hour? Perhaps you have decided to start a watch by yourself in your home. Maybe you will call a few friends and go from there. Or maybe you will contact your pastor about holding a watch. Whatever you do, you will become part of a large body of believers around the world who are watching until the Bridegroom comes.

The Watch of the Lord has always been envisioned by Bonnie and me as a global work of prayer. At no time have we seen it as limited to or confined by the borders of the United States or even North America. It's a worldwide work of prayer, a foundational element of God's plan to harvest the nations for His kingdom.

Our global vision for the Watch of the Lord is that of a fire that is spreading around the world. The Holy Spirit is the one who ignited it, and nothing can contain it or extinguish it. There should be watchmen crying out day and night for this nation and for the nations of the world. If the Lord gives grace, those who are keeping the watches in every town and city could carry those living embers of the watch to more nights each week. Maybe watches could last from the night to the next day to the next night. It would be glorious if the Watch of the Lord could go seven days a week, twenty-four hours a day.

But it's important to start where we are. We need to go in the strength we have, and the Lord will increase it. We can take a few bites now; we don't have to look at the whole cow! There are already a number of us watching and praying. God is now calling everyone to enlist in the Watch of the Lord and join together as global watchmen. He is calling us to function as priests before Him, to pray, weep and cry out for His glory to be released on earth. He is saying, "Watch with Me!"

All it takes is to share our vision for the Watch of the Lord and to make the commitment to watch and pray. Will you join us on the wall of prayer?

188

For thus saith the L<small>ORD</small> *of hosts;*
Yet once, it is a little while,
and I will shake the heavens, and the earth,
and the sea, and the dry land; and I will shake
all nations, and the desire of all nations shall come:
and I will fill this house with glory,
saith the L<small>ORD</small> *of hosts.*

—H<small>AGGAI</small> 2:6–7, <small>KJV</small>

13

It's Almost Midnight

NOT EVEN GOD Himself could sink this ship!" That was the boast of the captain of the *Titanic*. What an example of man's ultimate arrogance, of the futility of man trusting in himself rather than placing his confidence in the Lord Most High.

After all the money spent to impress the world's powerbrokers and make history by launching the most sumptuous ocean liner ever, after all the provision for comfort and pleasure and even the littlest of life's luxuries for the very rich on board, the White Star Line scrimped in an area that proved disastrous to rich and poor alike: They only installed enough lifeboats to accommodate half the passengers on board, so confident were the owners that the *Titanic* truly was "unsinkable."

That night ships at sea were aware of the position of the icebergs and had tried to warn the *Titanic* via the ship's wireless. One ship's operator aboard the *Californian* wired, "Say, old man, we are stopped and surrounded by ice." But an operator aboard the *Titanic*—busily trying to keep up with sending and receiving the numerous messages of her passengers—hastily wired back, "Shut up, shut up! I'm busy!"

The wireless operators were preoccupied with a lot of sound and fury, much ado about nothing. They were talking about Mrs. Astor's dog taking a stroll on the deck while the equipment that was given to them for real strategic purposes was being completely misused.

So the inevitable occurred. The *Titanic* struck a field of ice, and her sleek hull was ripped open. Her water-tight compartments quickly began to fill, and water spilled over from compartment to compartment. All the built-in safety measures eventually failed. The "unsinkable" *Titanic* was sinking.

OIL FOR THE LAMPS

IT WAS ALMOST midnight when the *Titanic* approached her appointment with disaster. That's probably about where we are today on God's timetable. The time is getting late for believers and unbelievers. The hour has come to grow into maturity.

Some believers have also neglected their lifeboats—the local churches. In the last days, we will need every lifeboat, just as the people on the *Titanic* needed them. Individual life jackets were not enough, because of the temperature of the water. They needed the lifeboats also, just as we do.

Our lifeboats, the local churches, need to be strong and healthy. Don't blow holes in the bottom of your boat by being divisive, gossipy, full of strife or by causing insurrection against God-appointed leaders. The purpose of God is that the watch will be a strength within every local church.

The people on board the *Titanic* were continuing their merriment in that late hour, just as the world is today. The wireless operators should have been using those instruments to save the ship, but they were just using them on frivolous messages. It's not only the world that is marching on oblivious to what's happening around them. Sometimes we, the church, are doing the same.

Our resources, like the wireless equipment aboard the *Titanic*, could be used for the Great Commission. Instead they are often spent on ourselves and our projects. The Spirit-filled church often regards the things of the prophetic as to be used just on themselves instead of in intercession for others. All too often we have used up our resources on useless things, just as the world has.

What is our duty now in this midnight hour? What is our assignment?

> Be dressed ready for service and keep your lamps burning, like men waiting for their master to return.... It will be good for those servants whose master finds them ready, even if he comes in the second or third watch of the night.
>
> —LUKE 12:35–36, 38, NIV

Yes, midnight is coming, but with the late hour comes our Lord! We must be watching and praying, with our lamps burning.

Remember the parable of the ten virgins that Jesus told. All the virgins, lamps in hand, went out to meet the bridegroom. All ten virgins began their vigil of watching wide awake, their lamps filled with plenty of oil, waiting expectantly for the bridegroom to appear. The five wise virgins took extra oil for their lamps; the five foolish virgins didn't.

However, the bridegroom was delayed.

> At midnight a cry was heard: "Behold, the bridegroom is coming; go out to meet him!"
>
> Then all those virgins arose and trimmed their lamps. And the foolish said to the wise, "Give us some of your oil, for our lamps are going out."
>
> —MATTHEW 25:6–8

The wise virgins knew they needed their own oil, and by the time the foolish virgins went to buy more for themselves, it was too late.

> The bridegroom came, and those who were ready went in with him to the wedding; and the door was shut.

> Afterward the other virgins came also, saying, "Lord, Lord, open to us!" But he answered and said, "Assuredly, I say to you, I do not know you."
>
> —MATTHEW 25:10–12

Only five virgins finished the vigil with enough oil for their lamps. Jesus then says, "Watch therefore . . . " (v. 13). We must keep our wicks trimmed and the oil of prayer in our lamps so the light of our faith is burning brightly when He comes.

OUR ASSIGNMENT: REMAIN ALERT AND VIGILANT

IN THE GARDEN of Gethsemane, the disciples could not stay awake "for sorrow" (Luke 22:45, KJV). Scientists have concluded in mind and body studies that sadness and grief hormonally and physiologically shut down the body's system, inducing sleep as an automatic attempt at preserving the mind and body in times of deep trauma.[1]

In order to remain alert, the disciples needed to resist their bodies' natural response to the terrible weight that had descended upon them—the knowledge that their Friend and Master was about to be sacrificed. They needed to resist sleep.

As the birth pangs of trouble ushering in the Lord's coming grow more intense, closer together and longer (just like those of a woman about to have a baby), we can anticipate that many will react to these sorrows by shutting down into a spiritual "sleep."

Jesus warned and exhorted against this continually, just as He exhorted His disciples in Gethsemane to wake up and pray! When everything prevails upon us to sleep, that is the time for vigilance!

Jesus urged His close disciples to watch and pray with Him in the Garden of Gethsemane. "Otherwise temptation will overpower you" (Luke 22:46, NLT). As a result of their spiritual drowsiness, they were not prepared for the testing that came later. The watch is "God's gym" where we develop spiritual muscle. We must be working out to develop our faith and prayer muscles to be ready for what comes.

194

OUR SPIRIT: LOVE AND GRACE

SOME PEOPLE ARE surprised to find out that we pray for the stabilization of the stock market and the world economy. We know that people's psychological condition affects how they buy and sell stocks; it governs the economic state of countries and the world. Whole nations can be affected, and the poor are affected the most when economies fail.

We know that some disasters are inevitable, but we are praying for good things to happen anyway. As long as there is economic stability, there will be resources to extend the gospel around the world. Until Jesus comes, the church's intercession should be for grace and mercy, not judgment or condemnation.

When a Samaritan village would not receive Jesus, His disciples James and John said, "Lord, do You want us to command fire to come down from heaven and consume them, just as Elijah did?" Jesus turned and rebuked them: "You do not know what manner of spirit you are of. For the Son of Man did not come to destroy men's lives but to save them" (Luke 9:54–56).

God in His time will do His part in judging sin; our part is to intercede. We need God's Spirit of compassion:

"As I live," says the Lord GOD, "I have no pleasure in the death
of the wicked, but that the wicked turn from his way and live."
—EZEKIEL 33:11

Beware of the prophet who comes in the spirit of delight over the death of "wicked persons"—the Old Testament term for New Testament "sinners." God is not relieved or happy to rid Himself of the unrighteous. His enemy is not people but the devil.

If God shows us a specific coming disaster, it is because He wants to instruct us on how to avert destruction in order that people may be saved from it. This was true in Abraham's day, Moses' day, Jonah's day, Daniel's day and Jesus' day—and it is true in our day.

The one specific coming—disaster—that Jesus prophesied was the destruction of the temple and the desolation of Jerusalem. He told everyone who listened what the specific signs would be, and then He gave them instructions: "When you see Jerusalem surrounded by armies, then know that its desolation is near. Then let those who are in Judea flee to the mountains, let those who are in the midst of her depart, and let not those who are in the country enter her" (Luke 21:20–21).

Jesus loved the people, so He told them how to save themselves as disaster struck. He knew there would be some who would want to stay in Jerusalem and resist the invasion. But in this case God said, "Get out."

Christians did exit when they saw these signs fulfilled in A.D. 70. They went to a small town, Pella, near the Sea of Galilee. The Jewish historian Josephus witnessed this second destruction of the temple and recounts it in his writings.

Our assignment is to love people and extend God's mercy to them. We are not here to condemn or gloat or judge others as the desolation and destruction draws closer. We are here to reveal the nature of Christ to a lost world.

OUR MIND-SET: PERSEVERANCE

AS WE ENTER the hour just before the glorious appearing of Christ, we understand from Scripture that the time ahead will be in preparation for a great conflict between the powers of light and darkness. Daily many signs around us agree with the Bible's testimony of our time. Jesus said ethnic groups would rise against ethnic groups. There would be earthquakes, famines, rampant diseases, fearful sights, great signs, persecution, imprisonment, betrayal and hatred. Men's hearts would fail them for all of these things. In the midst of this prophecy Jesus said, "In your patience possess ye your souls!" (Luke 21:9–28).

The church of this great hour will be renewed in full strength as it was from Pentecost through the first apostolic age. The Lord will manifest through her signs and wonders with great power, and there will be a great ingathering of souls in response to the message of the gospel.

As we look at our fathers of that first church age, we find a particular trait common to them that is all but absent in our generation. That trait, which must be restored if we are to fulfill God's foreordained purpose, is perseverance.

Perseverance is knitted to patience. *Perseverance* means "cheerful or hopeful endurance; constancy; to be constantly diligent; to attend diligently, with earnest care; giving regular attendance to all the exercises of something."

In our day in the church, God is gathering His "eagles" and massing His troops to resist satanic outpouring (Rev. 12:15–17). God's great army is being prepared to "take the prey," pulling down strongholds of evil supernatural resistance that are holding humanity in the bondage of sin and disease worldwide. We must develop perseverance, tenacity and biblical patience if we are to wage successful warfare!

When the Israelites came out of Egypt, they were promised blessing, but they had to fight for it. We, like the Israelites, may have to fight for every inch we obtain, because there are both demonic and carnal strongholds that always resist the Lord and those who are anointed by His Spirit! For centuries the church has given up claim to her inheritance. She has been in bondage, ineffective and overrun by the enemy. Now it is time for her to arise (Song of Sol. 2:10). We must perform the works of Jesus and refuse to turn back until He comes!

We are preparing to confront a fresh new set of challenges and realities. The battle between light and darkness is going to intensify. Gross darkness will cover the people (Isa. 60:2). But our challenge, corporately as the church, is to bring the glory down, to "arise, shine; for thy light is come, and the glory of the LORD is risen upon thee . . . and kings [will come] to the brightness of thy rising" (vv. 1–3, KJV). The darkness may get darker, but we will arise and shine in the world.

The Lord wants to teach us how to pave the way for revival and restoration within the church, and He wants it to spill out over all people in all nations. Our challenge is to bring the glory down so that those in darkness will see a great light—Jesus. If we are faithful, we can usher in a reformation that will change history.

But Satan's best strategy is to wear down the saints. He will always try to keep us focused on temporary details and circumstances, however minor, in order to distract our focus and direct our daily reserve toward that which does not profit us eternally. If possible, he will keep us looking inward at our own difficulties, hurts, pains, failures and disappointments, thereby keeping us in a defensive mode until we are drained and unfit for aggressive warfare against him.

Some Christians start on the road to victory and become casualties because they didn't realize the walk of faith was uphill. Jesus' walk to victory was up to Jerusalem, up to the Garden of Gethsemane and up the hill of Golgotha to the cross. Jesus said a wise king never goes to war without first "counting the cost." In other words, prepare beforehand to finish the fight.

Start moving. Don't delay. Don't be passive. Paul said that in a race, everyone competes, but only the one who crosses the line in victory gets the prize. The man who strives for the championship is temperate, wisely considering everything and ordering his life to lay hold of the prize (1 Cor. 9:24–25).

Our prize is an incorruptible, everlasting prize. Paul said, "Therefore I do not run like a man running aimlessly; I do not fight like a man beating the air" (v. 26, NIV). We must not fight as boxing the air. We have an objective, and we must have an eternal reward. We must get the Lord's strategy for the taking of every stronghold. We must persevere and press forward.

Our Attitude: Fear Not!

IN EVERY COMMISSION He gave, Jesus first said, "Fear not!" He usually followed that exhortation with another equally revealing one: "Don't get discouraged." Jesus' response to His disciples' specific question about disasters and the end of the age was: "Do not be terrified" (Luke 21:9). The Spirit of Christ will not engender fear or inspire or minister any panic of impending doom to His people. His voice will be clear, calm and practical. His first priority is to save—both souls and lives.

In Revelation we see a reference to some of the labor pains coming on the earth that bring about the return of Christ. "I looked, and behold, a black horse, and he who sat on it had a pair of scales in his hand. And I heard a voice in the midst of the four living creatures saying, 'A quart of wheat for a denarius, and three quarts of barley for a denarius'" (6:5–6).

That is ominous. Threatening. Frightening. Scarcity is coming wherein a day's wage will buy only a loaf of bread. But listen. This same Voice then commands the black horse and its rider: "Do not harm the oil and the wine" (v. 6). God will protect us in the midst of disaster.

As we see in the testing of Job, God—not the devil, not his demons, not man, righteous or unrighteous—retains ultimate control of the earth at all times. And even during the difficulties at the end of the age, the best portion will be reserved by God. For what? For whom? For those who know their God and do exploits (Dan. 11:32). Though they walk through the valley of impending doom, they fear no evil because He is present in their midst, and He prepares a banquet for them in the midst of their enemies (Ps. 23)!

Our perspective of difficult times must be that of our redemption through the blood of Jesus. Meanwhile, we have the down payment of the Holy Spirit (2 Cor. 1:22). In the same study of mind and body mentioned, the scientists state that love causes a person to experience "a general state of calm and contentment which facilitates cooperation," which is the "opposite of the fight or flight mobilization shared by fear and anger."[2]

Thus, our wise Captain of the Hosts is doing all He can now to cause His army to experience an atmosphere of assurance, love, joy and peace as we, His bride, watch with Him. He wants to calmly and gently prepare, instruct, motivate and commission us in the midst of great difficulty on the earth—without fear.

OUR CRY: SEND RAIN!

THE PICTURE PROVIDED for us in the Book of Joel is one of desolation.

There is no harvest. The barn is empty. The wheat has ceased. There is no wine. There is no oil. Why? Because there is no rain.

Many churches today exemplify such desolation. Souls are not being saved. There is no concern for the lost, the poor or the oppressed. Worship services are dry routine. The baptismal tank is empty. The altars are barren. Why? Because there is no rain.

"Lord, send rain!" We need the rain! Without it and the corporate vision inspired and anointed by the Holy Spirit, a church is destined to become ingrown, experience infighting and power struggles and eventually die. We need the rain! When it comes, life comes, along with a stirring and an awakening.

In this hour, the Lord is pointing out our desolation. We must be realistic enough to accept the fact that tremendous darkness is all around us. The people are in despair and in need of spiritual rain. Yes, we have experienced a few drops of the latter rain God promised to pour out on His people, but so much more is yet to come.

We need the rain—not just a few sprinkles, but showers. This is one of the purposes of the Watch of the Lord worldwide—to break through the demonic powers in the heavenlies and bring down the former and the latter rain. The Holy Spirit has begun to reveal the many areas laid waste by the enemy. Next, He will start the rebuilding process. But He needs willing intercessors in order to do it. He will restore power to His people.

We are experiencing some of the first drops of the promised "latter rain," but we still need to pray in the torrents. We are just in the beginning stage, and we cannot stop at this juncture. At the end of Joshua's career, after many successful battles, the Word of the Lord came to him: "There remains very much land yet to be possessed" (Josh. 13:1). That is the word for us today. We must yet possess our inheritance. And in order to do it, we need rain.

OUR DIRECTION: FULL SPEED AHEAD

THE FIRST MATE of the *Titanic* gave the order, "Turn away and slow," when faced with the impending collision with the iceberg. That's the

200

same order given by the church leadership today anytime trouble is spotted ahead. They put the brakes on, turn around and order those under their leadership to head in the opposite direction.

But sometimes the best strategy to avoid disaster is to plow straight ahead at full speed. If orders are given to either slow down or put it in reverse, it may prove to be the worst thing to do. If the *Titanic* had rammed the iceberg it may have fared better than it did trying to turn away. In turning away it took the hit broadside.

The Lord is saying to His church, "Don't be afraid! Regardless of what it looks like, full speed ahead! Don't turn back! Don't cut and run! Go forward!" If we countermand those orders in order to perhaps divert calamity, it may go worse for us, not better.

The Lord's voice in this hour is telling the church, our households, our families and our nation not to throw all the engines in reverse, get scared, run away or feel doom and gloom. If God is calling for a course correction, make the course correction, but with engines full steam ahead. A whole lot less damage and destruction will come that way.

ROW TOWARD THE WAVE

WE RECEIVED AN e-mail from friends who were praying for the safety of some TEAM missionaries who were in Papua, New Guinea, in July 1998 when the tidal wave hit, killing thousands. Within a day or two after the wave hit, these friends received an e-mail about what happened to those missionaries.

When the warning sounded and they knew a tidal wave was coming, the Lord laid it on their hearts to get into a boat and *row toward the wave*. All the Christians from those three villages got into their boats and began to row for their lives. The other villagers ran into the jungle.

Tidal waves are not crashing waves, but rise from underneath the water. The Christians had literally to row uphill in order to get to safety. They were able to crest the wave before it washed onshore. Then as the water came back out, their boats were pushed way out to sea. It took them a day to row back in. Only one Christian man was killed from those three villages. The rest survived.

Bonnie and I are called to awaken, equip and anoint the body of Christ to be in our place, ready for His coming. As deep darkness covers the earth, the church is going to arise and shine in all of God's glory. We will aggressively rise up in joy, light, worship, fullness, prosperity, healing, peace, spiritual warfare, authority, true revelation and overcoming the powers of darkness.

When the labor pangs of the earth announcing Jesus' coming are getting more intense, closer together and longer in terms of darkness and rumors and wars, the church won't retreat, but will row toward the wave. The missionaries in Papua, New Guinea, were given a strategy by God for victory that entailed going full speed ahead directly toward that which was threatening to destroy them; the strategy is the same for God's people here and now. Take courage from the Lord. If we fall, we must get up again and take as many people as we can in our "boat."

Do not be afraid of all the negative things being said about the future. Our God is right here with us—and in the future, too! Many negative things will be said that promote fear. The Lord said that as the end comes and things get worse, and "men's hearts [are] failing them from fear and the expectations of those things which are coming...," then we are to look up! "Lift up your heads, because your redemption draws near" (Luke 21:26, 28).

In the last days, Christians should be stable, anointed people who have the answers. The best way you can take care of your family in uncertain times is to be a watchman on the wall, to be alert and in the place of prayer and intercession. Part of the prescription Jesus gave for the last days was Mark 13:33–37.

We are going to be optimistic watchman—not depressed and defeated, but optimistic and courageous, knowing that the Lord is with us. I believe God wants us to be right in the middle of the battle—protected, with God at our side. Let's not think of running to the hills to escape. Instead, together let's row toward the wave.

Jesus does the greater things, that causes
my heart to sing, the opening up new doors, the
creator of mountains, hills, lakes & sea shore,
My conquering King over Babylon the Great Whore
He's who I live for. The resurrected
and living Savior, the Corrector of all bad behavior
My God and My King, My sword, shield,
& armor, my lifes partner, finisher & final
Author. He's my everything and always, the
true light & Father of all days. The God of
heaven & earth, the giver of Spirit, life,
and strength to give birth, My only ruler
in a world with no worth. He's God,
I'm God. The kind of King that sheds
blood for you, died for truth, gives you bread
by the morning dew, & by My voice says God
I'll break you through O Son of David I'm
forever with you. Says He that is
        Faithful and forever True, I'm God

§

He will not let your foot slip—
he who watches over you will not slumber;
indeed, he who watches over Israel
will neither slumber nor sleep.

—PSALM 121:3–4, NIV

14

A Blessing
for the Watch

§

THE PROPHET JOEL called for corporate prayer and fasting when the nation of Israel was in peril (Joel 1:13–14). The people humbled themselves in prayer, watching, fasting and worship, and the Lord heard their prayers and delivered them. Joel called the people onto the wall of prayer, and today the Spirit is still calling those who will hear His cries for His people to come to their stations on the wall of prayer.

Around the world watchmen are running on the wall of intercession, entering the doors and windows of the enemy's camp and spending that time in prayer and warfare in order to take back all that the enemy has stolen from their lives and from the lives of their loved ones. "Proclaim this among the nations: 'Prepare for war! Wake up the mighty men, let all the men of war draw near, let them come up . . . let the weak say, I am strong'" (Joel 3:9–10).

At present we have hundreds of watches linked to us around the world. We invite you to join our ranks and link shields with us. Jehovah Sabbaoth—the Captain of the armies—wants you. Will you enlist?

The watch doesn't belong to us; it's the Lord's. We want to pass it on from where the fire has fallen. The Lord has graciously restored the watch in our era. It's living. Now we want to give it to others.

These stanzas from "Hymns for the Watch-Night," written by Charles Wesley in the 1700s, have become alive for today's watchmen:

Oft have we pass'd the guilty night,
In revellings and frantic mirth:
The creature was our sole delight,
Our happiness the things of earth;
But O! suffice the season past,
We choose the better part at last.

We will not close our wakeful eyes,
We will not let our eyelids sleep,
But humbly lift them to the skies,
And all a solemn vigil keep:
So many years on sin bestow'd
Can we not watch one night for God?

For ever let th' Archangel's voice
Be sounding in our ears
The solemn midnight cry,
"Ye dead, the Judge is come!
Arise and meet him in the sky,
And meet your instant doom!"

O may we thus be found,
Obedient to his word,
Attentive to the trumpet's sound,
And looking for our Lord!
O may we thus ensure
Our lot among the blest,
And watch a moment to secure
An everlasting rest![1]

A Blessing for the Watch

The Lord Your Watchman

ABOVE ALL, REMEMBER that God is the premier Watchman.

> I will lift up my eyes to the hills—from whence comes my help? My help comes from the LORD, who made heaven and earth. He will not allow your foot to be moved. He who keeps you will not slumber. Behold, He who keeps Israel shall neither slumber nor sleep.
>
> —PSALM 121:1–3

The Lord watches over you. He is your strength and your shield (Ps. 28:7). The Lord is the chief Watchman. He watches over His flock like a shepherd (Jer. 31:10). Lean into Him. Trust in His care and His overwhelming love for you.

Prayer and Blessing

IF YOU ARE feeling drawn by the Holy Spirit to join us on the wall of prayer as we watch all night together, will you pray with us?

Father, thank You for drawing Your people to watch with us on the wall. Thank You, Lord, that You have revealed the urgent nature of watching in prayer in this hour. Thank You, Father, that Your hand is upon this reader right now and that this reader has taken to heart the call to join us on the wall of intercession.

Lord, activate the vision of the Watch of the Lord in the heart of this reader. Cover this one with Your hand of blessing and protection so that the vision is accomplished and not stolen. That which You have planted, water and bring to life. Bring this dear watchman into the full stature of Your plan.

Cause Your blessing to be upon the small things so that together we may accomplish a great and mighty global work that will release Your glory on the earth. In Jesus' name we pray. Amen.

Notes

CHAPTER 2
THE WATCH IN SCRIPTURE

1. *Websters Collegiate Dictionary,* 10th ed., s.v. "watch."

CHAPTER 4
THE WALL OF PRAYER

1. Nehemiah Curnack, ed., volume 2 of *The Journal of the Rev. John Wesley A.M,* 8 vols. (London: Epworth, 1938), 122.
2. Eddie L. Hyatt, *2000 Years of Charismatic Christianity* (Tulsa, OK: Hyatt International Ministries, Inc., 1996), 153.

CHAPTER 8
PROPHETIC WATCHMEN

1. Thomas Conklin, *The Titanic Sinks* (New York: Random House, 1997), n.p.
2. John J. Lumpkin, "God Helped Him Eject, Stealth Pilot Says," *Albuquerque Journal,* 6 April 1999, from Internet site www.albqjournal.com /news/1news04–06
3. "14 hurt by bomb at French school; many saved by bell," the *Charlotte Observer,* September 8, 1995, obtained from Internet

source at http://newslibrary.infi.net/global/cgi-bin/char/slwe-bcli_get.pl?DBLIST=CO95+DOCNUM=41786

CHAPTER 9
THE WATCH AND ISRAEL

1. Internet source at www.jewishpost.com for The Jewish Post of New York Online for October 9, 1996.

CHAPTER 10
LINE UPON LINE, PRECEPT UPON PRECEPT

1. Stephen Mansfield, *Never Give In: The Extraordinary Character of Winston Churchill* (Elkton, MD: Holly Hall Publications, 1995), n.p.

CHAPTER 12
GOD PLUS ONE IS A MAJORITY

1. Excerpt of speech titled "Too Few" given by Winston Churchill, House of Commons, August 20, 1940
2. Geoffrey Brooks, *Hitler's Nuclear Weapons: The Development and Attempted Deployment of Radiological Armaments by Nazi Germany* (London: Leo Cooper, 1992), n.p.

CHAPTER 13
IT'S ALMOST MIDNIGHT

1. Daniel Goldman, *Emotional Intelligence* (New York: Bantam Books, 1995), 7
2. Ibid.

CHAPTER 14
A BLESSING FOR THE WATCH

1. Charles Wesley, *Hymns for the Watch-Night*, public domain.

How to Contact Us

Mahesh Chavda Ministries International
P.O. Box 472009
Charlotte, NC 28247
Phone: (704) 543-7272
Fax: (704) 541-5300

E-mail: info@watchofthelord.com
www.watchofthelord.com

Note: As doctors in our area started sending severely ill cancer patients to our watches, we realized that our watch hours needed to change to accommodate them. We were arriving at the church for the 10 P.M. watch to find them waiting in line to get into the church building. The Lord moved our hearts to start the watch earlier to serve them, so they could be prayed for earlier. For the present we start the watch at 7:30 P.M. Our watch times are subject to change by the Lord's leading.

As you take up the call to watch
and pray, you will be strengthened by looking us
up on our Web site, www.watchofthelord.com,
where you will get further up-to-date
information on the Watch of the Lord.
We encourage you to come and experience the watch
at our base especially during our conferences.
The dates will be posted on our Web site or you may
inquire by phone, fax or mail.

WE ENCOURAGE YOU TO GET OTHER RESOURCE MATERIAL FROM OUR MINISTRY, INCLUDING:

- *Only Love Can Make a Miracle:* A treasury of testimonies, including the raising of a six-year-old boy from the dead.

- *The Hidden Power of Prayer and Fasting:* Keys that will unlock the resident power of the Holy Spirit within you!

- *A Visit to Heaven:* The exciting story of an African woman's heavenly visit.

OASIS BIBLE STUDY:

- Thirty-one studies designed to help Christians apply the Bible to their lives.

ANOINTED AUDIO TAPES INCLUDE:

- *Watch of the Lord* (Mahesh & Bonnie Chavda): These tapes will equip you in the work of prayer.

- *Prayer and Fasting* (Mahesh Chavda): Guidelines assisting committed intercessors and spiritual warriors with battle weapons.

- *Promise, Power and Purpose of Pentecost* (Mahesh Chavda): Three inspiring messages on how to walk in the promises, power and purposes of God.

- *Daughter of the Lion Is a Lion* (Bonnie Chavda): A delightful journey that reveals the Lion of Judah conquering our adversary.

- *Open Windows to Heaven* (Bonnie Chavda): A call to corporate prayer.

For additional material, please send for our catalog.

You can experience more of God's grace & love!